HOW TO Write Business Letters

Gaurav Shah

4735/22, Prakash Deep Building
Ansari Road, Darya Ganj,
New Delhi - 110002

Lotus Press : Publishers & Distributors
Unit No. 220, 2nd Floor, 4735/22, Prakash Deep Building,
Ansari Road, Darya Ganj, New Delhi- 110002
Ph.: 41325510, 98118-38000
• E-mail : lotuspress1984@gmail.com
www.lotuspress.co.in

How to Write Business Letters

ISBN: 81-8382-187-1

Printed & Published by : **Lotus Press Publisher & Distributors,** New Delhi-02

PREFACE

Letter writing is one of the oldest modes of communication. Tough in today's time of technological advancement letter writing has lost its charm to a great extent but it remains an important tool in some walks of life especially in business. Business letters are still very effective in maintaining good relations or getting good orders. A business letter is a formal way of communicating between two or more parties. There are many different uses and types of business letters. Business letters can be informational, persuasive, motivational, or promotional.

Writing for a business audience is usually quite different than writing in the humanities, social sciences, or other academic disciplines. Business writing strives to be crisp and succinct rather than evocative or creative; it stresses specificity and accuracy. This distinction does not make business writing superior or inferior to other styles. Rather, it reflects the unique purpose and considerations involved when writing in a business context.

Business writing varies from the conversational style often found in email messages to the more formal, legalistic style found in contracts. A style between these two extremes is appropriate for the majority of memos, emails, and letters. Writing that is too formal can alienate readers, and an attempt to be overly casual may come across as insincere or unprofessional. In business writing, as in all writing, one must know their audience. In most cases, the business letter will be the first impression that you make on someone. Though business writing has become less formal over time, one should still take great care that the letter's content should be clear so that it can make a sound impression and helps to achieve its aim.

Business letters can be of several types. Acknowledgement letters, acceptance letters, congratulation letters, demand and denial letters, explanation letters, legal letters, revenue letters, employer and employee related letters, promotional letters, thanks letters, request letters etc. are some kind of letters which are frequently used in various businesses. Some business letters tends to be short while some letters need complete explanations. But a majority of business letters are not very long and time taking. In writing a business letter one has to be very precise about the text and its length. The length of a business letter should not exceed the tolerable limit otherwise it will not solve its purpose.

The language of a business letter should be pragmatic and easy to understand so that it can easily interpret its meaning. The present book is a collection of many such business letters which can be of great importance in today's life. We hope that this book will be thoroughly enjoyed by the readers of different class and age and it will help them in climbing the success ladder in today's competitive environment.

Author

CONTENTS

1

Business Letters

Business letters are required in many different situations, from applying for a job to requesting or delivering information. Despite the widespread use of e-mail in commerce today, traditional business letters are still the main way that the majority of businesses officially communicate with their customers and other businesses.

This is especially true when businesses want to formalize an agreement or an understanding. So far, emails are great for all of the preparatory work, but a formal business letter is still most often needed to "seal the deal".

Importance of commercial correspondence

Commercial correspondence is the correspondence you share with another party during the course of or in continuation of a business transaction. It is a very important part of business, primarily because it is a form of written documentation of the client's requirements, your statement of intent and ability, and all the other things, good and bad, associated with a business transaction.

Commercial correspondence can address different issues or modules of a business cycle. It could be a letter from the client stating what they need, or a letter from you to the client stating any specific items you wanted discussed in a meeting, for instance.

Commercial correspondence is not only important to business; it is a critical aspect of business. Commercial correspondence acts as a reference point for any queries regarding a project completed in the past. There can be different kinds of commercial correspondence — a requirement document, a courtesy letter, a complaint letter, etc.

No one can deny the importance of business letters in the world of commerce. The success of any modern business depends on the use of business letters. Good letters are little ambassadors that traverse every corner of the present day commercial world. They constitute the biggest source of active liaison that is necessary concomitant for producing business.

Correspondence is the first step in breaking the ice between business houses or the customer and the business house to achieve the desired goal. In present days, commerce and trade have extended to such a great space, as it has become impossible for a businessman to have direct conversation with his customers and suppliers. Contact can be made between the manufacturer and the trade without any personal meeting through correspondence. Personal contacts involve money, time and energy the precious properties of business house, which could be easily saved by resorting to correspondence.

It is said that correspondence keeps the relations alive. Even if persons do not meet each other they can feel the presence through correspondence. In case of a business, the relationship can be strengthened by frequent correspondence. Suppose a trader is to pay to the supplier on a particular date. If he fails, the supplier may be worried and lose confidence in him. But the trader writes in advance expressing his inability to meet the obligation on the specified date. It will create confidence in the mind of the supplier and future credit will not be a problem.

Types of business letters

There are two basic categories of business letters: business to business, and business to customer.

Business to Business Letters

Most business to business letters are written to confirm things that have already been discussed among officials in meetings, on the telephone, or via e-mail.

Can you imagine the letters that would have to go back and forth to cover all of the questions and possibilities that can be covered in a one-hour meeting, a half-hour phone call, or a few quick e-mails?

The main purpose of a typical business letter is to formalize the details that were arrived at in those discussions, and to provide any additional information that was agreed upon.

Over the years, certain general standards have evolved in the business world that the vast majority of businesses use in drafting their business to business correspondence.

Business to Customer Letters

There are many different types of business to customer letters. They include: sales and marketing letters, information letters, order acknowledgement letters, order status letters, collection letters, among others.

As with business to business letters, over the years certain general standards have evolved in the business world that the vast majority of businesses use in drafting letters to existing and potential customers.

Of course, going in the other direction are customer to business letters. These include: order letters, order status inquiry letters, complaint letters, and others.

Since these are customer-generated letters, there is no particular expectation that they follow any particular letter-writing standard. Typically, they are handled just like any other piece of personal correspondence.

Parts of a Business Letter

Date

The date line is used to indicate the date the letter was written. However, if your letter is completed over a number of days, use the date it was finished in the date line. When writing to companies within the United States, use the American date format. (The United States-based convention for formatting a date places the month before the day. For example: June 11, 2001.) Write out the month, day and year two inches from the top of the page. Depending which format you are using for your letter, either left justify the date or center it horizontally.

Sender's Address

Including the address of the sender is optional. If you choose to include it, place the address one line below the date. Do not write the sender's name or title, as it is included in the letter's closing. Include only the street address, city and pin code. Another option is to include the sender's address directly after the closing signature.

Inside Address

The inside address is the recipient's address. It is always best to write to a specific individual at the firm to which you are writing. If you do not have the person's name, do some research by calling the company or speaking with employees from the company. Include a personal title such as Ms., Mrs., Mr., or Dr. Follow a woman's preference in being addressed as Miss, Mrs., or Ms. If you are unsure of a woman's preference in being addressed, use Ms. If there is a possibility that the person to whom you are writing is a Dr. or has some other title, use that title. Usually, people will not mind being addressed by a higher title than they actually possess. For international addresses, type the name of the country in all-capital letters on the last line. The inside address begins one line below the sender's address or one inch below the date. It should be left justified, no matter which format you are using.

Salutation

Use the same name as the inside address, including the personal title. If you know the person and typically address them by their first name, it is acceptable to use only the first name in the salutation (for example: Dear Lalitha). In all other cases, however, use the personal title and full name followed by a colon. Leave one line blank after the salutation.

If you don't know a reader's gender, use a nonsexist salutation, such as "To Whom it May Concern." It is also acceptable to use the full name in a salutation if you cannot determine gender. For example, you might write Dear Chris Harmon: if you were unsure of Chris's gender.

Body

For block and modified block formats, single space and left justify each paragraph within the body of the letter. Leave a blank line between each paragraph. When writing a business letter, be careful to remember that conciseness is very important. In the first paragraph, consider a friendly opening and then a statement of the main point. The next paragraph should begin justifying the importance of the main point. In the next few paragraphs, continue justification with background information and supporting details. The closing paragraph should restate the purpose of the letter and, in some cases, request some type of action.

Closing

The closing begins at the same horizontal point as your date and one line after the last body paragraph. Capitalize the first word only (for example: Thank you) and leave four lines between the closing and the sender's name for a signature. If a colon follows the salutation, a comma should follow the closing; otherwise, there is no punctuation after the closing.

Enclosures

If you have enclosed any documents along with the letter, such as a resume, you indicate this simply by typing Enclosures one line below the closing. As an option, you may list the name of each document you are including in the envelope. For instance, if you have included many documents and need to ensure that the recipient is aware of each document, it may be a good idea to list the names.

Principles to keep in mind

Business writing is different

Writing for a business audience is usually quite different than writing in the humanities, social sciences, or other academic disciplines. Business writing strives to be crisp and succinct rather than evocative or creative; it stresses specificity and accuracy. This distinction does not make business writing superior or inferior to other styles. Rather, it reflects the unique purpose and considerations involved when writing in a business context.

When you write a business document, you must assume that your audience has limited time in which to read it and is likely to skim. Your readers have an interest in what you say insofar as it affects their working world. They want to know the "bottom line": the point you are making about a situation or problem and how they should respond.

Business writing varies from the conversational style often found in email messages to the more formal, legalistic style found in contracts. A style between these two extremes is appropriate for the majority of memos, emails, and letters. Writing that is too formal can alienate readers, and an attempt to be overly casual may come across as insincere or unprofessional. In business writing, as in all writing, you must know your audience.

In most cases, the business letter will be the first impression that you make on someone. Though business writing has become less formal over time, you should still take great care that your letter's content is clear and that you have proofread it carefully.

Pronouns and active versus passive voice

Personal pronouns (like I, we, and you) are important in letters and memos. In such documents, it is perfectly appropriate to refer to yourself as I and to the reader as you. Be careful, however, when you use the pronoun we in a business letter that is written on company stationery, since it commits your company to what you have written. When stating your opinion, use I; when presenting company policy, use we.

The best writers strive to achieve a style that is so clear that their messages cannot be misunderstood. One way to achieve a clear style is to minimize your use of the passive voice. Although the passive voice is sometimes necessary, often it not only makes your writing dull but also can be ambiguous or overly impersonal. Here's an example of the same point stated in passive voice and in the active voice:

PASSIVE: The net benefits of subsidiary divestiture were grossly overestimated.

[Who did the overestimating?]

ACTIVE: The Global Finance Team grossly overestimated the net benefits of subsidiary divestiture.

The second version is clearer and thus preferable.

Of course, there are exceptions to every rule. What if you are the head of the Global Finance

Team? You may want to get your message across without calling excessive attention to the fact that the error was your team's fault. The passive voice allows you to gloss over an unflattering point—but you should use it sparingly.

Focus and specificity

Business writing should be clear and concise. Take care, however, that your document does not turn out as an endless series of short, choppy sentences. Keep in mind also that "concise" does not have to mean "blunt"—you still need to think about your tone and the audience for whom you are writing. Consider the following examples:

After carefully reviewing this proposal, we have decided to prioritize other projects this quarter.

Nobody liked your project idea, so we are not going to give you any funding.

The first version is a weaker statement, emphasizing facts not directly relevant to its point. The second version provides the information in a simple and direct manner. But you don't need to be an expert on style to know that the first phrasing is diplomatic and respectful (even though it's less concise) as compared with the second version, which is unnecessarily harsh and likely to provoke a negative reaction.

Business letters: where to begin

Reread the description of your task (for example, the advertisement of a job opening, instructions for a proposal submission, or assignment prompt for a course). Think about your purpose and what requirements are mentioned or implied in the description of the task. List these requirements.

This list can serve as an outline to govern your writing and help you stay focused, so try to make it thorough. Next, identify qualifications, attributes, objectives, or answers that match the requirements you have just listed. Strive to be exact and specific, avoiding vagueness, ambiguity, and platitudes. If there are industry- or field-specific concepts or terminology that are relevant to the task at hand, use them in a manner that will convey your competence and experience.

Avoid any language that your audience may not understand. Your finished piece of writing should indicate how you meet the requirements you've listed and answer any questions raised in the description or prompt.

Some tips on business letters

A business letter is more formal than a personal letter. It should have a margin of at least one inch on all four edges. It is always written on 8½"x11" (or metric equivalent) unlined stationery. There are six parts to a business letter.

The Heading

This contains the return address (usually two or three lines) with the date on the last line.

Sometimes it may be necessary to include a line after the address and before the date for a phone number, fax number, e-mail address, or something similar.

Often a line is skipped between the address and date. That should always be done if the heading is next to the left margin.

It is not necessary to type the return address if you are using stationery with the return address already imprinted. Always include the date.

The Inside Address

This is the address you are sending your letter to. Make it as complete as possible. Include titles and names if you know them.

This is always on the left margin. If an 8½" x 11" paper is folded in thirds to fit in a standard 9" business envelope, the inside address can appear through the window in the envelope.

An inside address also helps the recipient route the letter properly and can help should the envelope be damaged and the address become unreadable.

Skip a line after the heading before the inside address. Skip another line after the inside address before the greeting.

The Greeting

Also called the salutation. The greeting in a business letter is always formal. It normally begins with the word "Dear" and always includes the person's last name.

It normally has a title. Use a first name only if the title is unclear—for example, you are writing to someone named "Lalita," but do not know whether the person is male or female.

The greeting in a business letter always ends in a colon. (You know you are in trouble if you get a letter from a boyfriend or girlfriend and the greeting ends in a colon—it is not going to be friendly.)

The Body

The body is written as text. A business letter is never hand written. Depending on the letter style you choose, paragraphs may be indented. Regardless of format, skip a line between paragraphs.

Skip a line between the greeting and the body. Skip a line between the body and the close.

The Complimentary Close

This short, polite closing ends with a comma. It is either at the left margin or its left edge is in the center, depending on the Business Letter Style that you use. It begins at the same column the heading does.

The block style is becoming more widely used because there is no indenting to bother with in the whole letter.

The Signature Line

Skip two lines (unless you have unusually wide or narrow lines) and type out the name to be signed. This customarily includes a middle initial, but does not have to. Women may indicate how they wish to be addressed by placing Miss, Mrs., Ms. or similar title in parentheses before their name.

The signature line may include a second line for a title, if appropriate. The term "By direction" in the second line means that a superior is authorizing the signer.

The signature should start directly above the first letter of the signature line in the space between the close and the signature line. Use blue or black ink. Business letters should not contain postscripts.

Application letters and cover letters

Many people believe that application letters and cover letters are essentially the same. For purposes of this handout, though, these kinds of letters are different. The letter of application is a sales letter in which you market your skills, abilities, and knowledge. A cover letter, on the other hand, is primarily a document of transmittal. It identifies an item being sent, the person to whom it is being sent, and the reason for its being sent, and provides a permanent record of the transmittal for both the writer and the reader.

Application letters

When writing an application letter, remember that you probably have competition. Your audience is a professional who screens and hires job applicants—someone who may look through dozens or even hundreds of other applications on the day she receives yours. The immediate objective of your application letter and accompanying resume is to attract this person's attention. Your ultimate goal is to obtain an interview.

As you write your application letter, be sure you complete three tasks: catch the reader's attention favourably, convince the reader that you are a qualified candidate for the job, and request an interview.

Application letter checklist

- Identify the job by title and let the recipient know how you heard about it.
- Summarize your qualifications for the job, specifically your work experience, activities that show your leadership skills, and your educational background.
- Refer the reader to your enclosed resume.
- Ask for an interview, stating where you can be reached and when you will be available. If your prospective employer is located in another city and you plan to visit the area, mention the dates for your trip.
- If you are applying for a specific job, include any information pertinent to the position that is not included in your resume.
- To save your reader time and to call attention to your strengths as a candidate, state your objective directly at the beginning of the letter.

Example: I am seeking a position as a manager in your Data Center. In such a management position, I can use my master's degree in information systems and my experience as a programmer/ analyst to address business challenges in data processing.

If you have been referred to a company by one of its employees, a career counselor, a professor, or someone else, mention that before stating your job objective.

Example: During the recent convention in Delhi, one of your sales representatives, informed me of a possible opening for a manager in your Data Center. My extensive background in programming and my master's degree in information systems make me highly qualified for the position.

In subsequent paragraphs, expand on the qualifications you mentioned in your opening. Add any appropriate details, highlighting experience listed on your resume that is especially pertinent to the job you are seeking. Close with a request for an interview. Proofread your letter carefully.

Two sample letters of application are presented below. The first letter (Sample #1) is by a recent college graduate responding to a local newspaper article about the company's plan to build a new computer center. The writer is not applying for a specific job opening but describes the position he seeks. The second letter (Sample #2) is from a college student who does not specify where he learned of the opening because he is uncertain whether a position is available.

Sample 1

61/23 Mahatma Gandhi Road
Apartment B-11
Bangalore
January 11, 2005
Phoenix India Ltd,
69/4 Industrial Lane
Dehradun,

Dear Human Resources Director,

I just read an article in a reputed daily about your new computer center just north of Dehradun. I would like to apply for a position as an entry-level programmer at the center.

I understand that your company produces both in-house and customer documentation. My technical writing skills, as described in the enclosed resume, are well suited to your company. I am a recent graduate of D. J. Institute of Technology with an Associate's Degree in Computer Science. In addition to having taken a broad range of courses, I served as a computer consultant at the college's computer center where I helped train users to work with new systems.

I will be happy to meet with you at your convenience and discuss how my education and experience match your needs.

Yours Sincerely,

Ravikant Tewari

Sample 2

61/23 Mahatma Gandhi Road
Apartment B-11
Bangalore
January 11, 2005
Phoenix India Ltd,
69/4 Industrial Lane
Dehradun,

Dear Ms. Kapoor,

I am seeking a position in your engineering department where I may use my training in computer sciences to solve Phoenix India Ltd's engineering problems. I would like to be a part of the department that developed the Internet Selection System but am unsure whether you have a current opening.

I expect to receive a Bachelor of Science degree in Engineering from D. J. Institute of Technology in June and by that time will have completed the Computer Systems Engineering Program.

Since September 2000, I have been participating, through the University, in the Professional Training Programme at Computer Systems International in Bangalore. In the programme I was assigned to several staff sections as an apprentice. Most recently, I have been a programmer trainee in the Engineering Department and have gained a great deal of experience in computer applications. Details of the academic courses I have taken are included in the enclosed resume.

If there is a position open at your company, please let me know whom I should contact for further information. I look forward to hearing from you soon.

Yours Sincerely,

Ravikant Tewari

Cover Letters

As mentioned previously, application letters and cover letters are not the same. A cover letter identifies an item being sent, the person to whom it is being sent, and the reason for its being sent. A cover letter provides a permanent record of the transmittal for both the writer and the reader.

In a cover letter, keep your remarks brief. Your opening should explain what you are sending and why. In an optional second paragraph, you might include a summary of the information you are sending. A letter accompanying a proposal, for example, might point out sections in the proposal that might be of particular interest to the reader. The letter could then go on to present a key point or two explaining why the writer's firm is the best one for the job.

The closing paragraph should contain acknowledgements, offer additional assistance, or express the hope that the material will fulfill its purpose.

The following are examples of cover letters. The first letter (Sample #1) is brief and to the point. The second letter (Sample #2) is slightly more detailed because it touches on the manner in which the information was gathered.

Sample 1

Your Company Logo and Contact Information
January 12, 2008
Rohit Khanna,
Chief Engineer
Sky Chemical Products
23/7, Street 8,
Pune

Dear Mr. Khanna,

Enclosed is the final report on our installment of pollution control equipment at Chemical Company, which we send with company's permission.

Please call me or email me at the address below if I can answer any questions.

Sincerely,

Rajesh Taneja
Technical Services Manager
1234@company.com
Enclosure: Report

Sample 2

Your Company Logo and Contact Information
January 12, 2008
Rohit Khanna,
Chief Engineer
Sky Chemical Products
23/7, Street 8,
Pune

Dear Mr. Khanna,

Enclosed is the report estimating our power consumption for the year as requested by Mr. Roy, Vice President, on December 4, 2007.

The report is the result of several meetings with Lalit Gautam, Manager of Plant Operations, and his staff and an extensive survey of all our employees. The survey was delayed by the transfer of key staff in Building A. We believe, however, that the report will provide the information you need to furnish us with a cost estimate for the installation of your Energy Saving System.

If you need more information, please let me know.

Sincerely,

Rajesh Taneja
Technical Services Manager
1234@company.com
Enclosure: Report

Guide to Basic Business Letters

The Basics

The basics of good business letter writing are easy to learn. The following guide provides the phrases that are usually found in any standard business letter. These phrases are used as a kind of frame and introduction to the content of business letters.

At the end of this guide, you will find links to sites that give tips on the difficult part of writing successful business letters — arguing your business objective. By using these standard phrases, you can give a professional tone to your English business letters.

The Start

Dear Personnel Director,

Dear Sir or Madam: (use if you don't know who you are writing to)

Dear Dr, Mr, Mrs, Miss or Ms Smith: (use if you know who you are writing to, and have a formal relationship with — very important use Ms for women unless asked to use Mrs or Miss)

Dear Feroze: (use if the person is a close business contact or friend)

The Reference

With reference to your advertisement in the Times, your letter of 23rd March,

your phone call today,

Thank you for your letter of March 5th. Unfortunately

I am afraid that

Enclosing Documents

I am enclosing

Please find enclosed

Enclosed you will find

Closing Remarks

Thank you for your help. Please contact us again if we can help in any way.

there are any problems.

you have any questions.

Reference to Future Contact

I look forward to ...

hearing from you soon.

meeting you next Tuesday.

seeing you next Thursday.

The Finish

Yours faithfully, (If you don't know the name of the person you're writing to)

Yours Sincerely, (If you know the name of the person you're writing to)

Best wishes,

Best regards, (If the person is a close business contact or friend)

Sample Letter

Here is a sample letter using some of these forms:

January 12, 2008
Rohit Khanna,
Chief Engineer
Sky Chemical Products
23/7, Street 8, Pune

Dear Mr. Khanna,

With reference to our telephone conversation today, I am writing to confirm your order Ref. No. 234. The order will be shipped within three days and should arrive at your store in about 10 days.

Please contact us again if we can help in any way.

Rajesh Taneja
Technical Services Manager
1234@company.com

More Detailed Help with Business Letters

Business Letter Writing: Enquiries — Asking for Information

We write an enquiry when we want to ask for more information concerning a product, service or other information about a product or service that interests us. These letters are often written in response to an advertisement that we have seen in the paper, a magazine, a commercial on television when we are interested in purchasing a product, but would like more information before making a decision.

Remember to place your or your company's address at the top of the letter (or use your company's letterhead) followed by the address of the company you are writing to. The date can either be placed double spaced down or to the right.

Important Language to Remember

The Start: Dear Sir or Madam

To Whom It May Concern — (very formal as you do not know the person to whom you are writing)

Giving Reference: With reference to your advertisement (ad) in...

Regarding your advertisement (ad) in ...

Requesting a Catalogue, Brochure, Etc.: After the reference, add a comma and continue - ... , would (Could) you please send me ...

Requesting Further Information: I would also like to know ...

Could you tell me whether ...

Signature: Yours faithfully — (very formal as you do not know the person to whom you are writing)

An example letter

Rajesh Taneja
Technical Services Manager
1234@company.com
July 12, 2008

Dear Mr. Taneja,

With reference to your advertisement in yesterday's newspaper, could you please send me a copy of your latest catalogue. I would also like to know if it is possible to make purchases online.

Yours Faithfully

(Signature)
Amit Vaishya
Vice President
ABC systems

Responding to Inquiries and Requests for Information

It is very important to make a good impression when responding to inquiries from potential customers. Of course, the best impression will be made by providing the materials or information that the perspective client has asked for, this positive impression will be improved by a well written response.

Remember to place your or your company's address at the top of the letter (or use your company's letterhead) followed by the address of the company you are writing to. The date can either be placed double spaced down or to the right. You can also include a reference number for correspondence.

Important Language to Remember

The Start:

Dear Mr, Ms (Mrs, Miss very important use Ms for women unless asked to use Mrs or Miss)

Thanking the Potential Customer for His/Her Interest:

Thank you for your letter of ... inquiring (asking for information) about ...

We would like to thank you for your letter of ... inquiring (asking for information) about ...

Providing Requested Materials:

We are pleased to enclose ...

Enclosed you will find ...

We enclose ...

Providing Additional Information:

We would also like to inform you ...

Regarding your question about ...

In answer to your question (inquiry) about ...

Closing a Letter Hoping for Future Business:

We look forward to ... hearing from you / receiving your order / welcoming you as our client (customer).

Signature:

Yours Sincerely (remember use 'Yours faithfully' when you don't know the name of the person you are writing and 'Yours Sincerely' when you do.

An example letter

Rajesh Taneja
Technical Services Manager
1234@company.com

Mr. Taneja,

Thank you for your inquiry of 12 July asking for the latest edition of our catalogue.

We are pleased to enclose our latest brochure. We would also like to inform you that it is possible to make purchases online at www. company. com.

We look forward to welcoming you as our customer.

Yours Sincerely,

(Signature)
Lalit Khanna

Account Terms and Conditions

The following letter outlines the terms of a newly opened business account.

Useful Key Phrases

Thank you for opening an account with...

I would like to take this opportunity ...

Invoices are payable within ...

As..., I will be happy to answer any questions you may have regarding...

...and therefore encourage the use of...

We consider this incentive...

An example letter

Dear Amit,

Thank you for opening an account with our company. As one of the leaders in this industry, we can assure you that our products and our services will not disappoint you.

I would like to take this opportunity to briefly set forth our terms and conditions for maintaining an open account with our firm. Invoices are payable within 30 days of receipt, with a 2% discount available if your payment is remitted within ten (10) days of receipt.

We consider this incentive an excellent opportunity for our customers to increase their profit margin, and therefore encourage the use of this discount privilege whenever possible. We do, however, require that our invoices be paid within the specified time, for our customers to take advantage of this 2% discount.

At various times throughout the year we may offer our customers additional discounts on our products. In determining your cost in this case, you must apply your special discount first, and then calculate your 2% discount for early payment.

As the credit manager, I will be happy to answer any questions you may have regarding your new account. I can be reached at the my number, 3452567. Welcome to our family of customers.

Yours Sincerely,

Narendra Rajan

Credit Manager,

Apex Bank Corporations

Business meetings

The following dialogue is an example of a typical business meeting. As you can see from the dialogue, a typical business meeting can be divided into five parts:

This example business meeting is followed by the two sections which provide key language and phrases appropriate for typical business meetings.

Introductions

Meeting Chairman: If we are all here, let's get started. First of all, I'd like you to please join me in welcoming V. Shankar, our new Area Sales Vice President.

V. Shankar: Thank you for having me, I'm looking forward to today's meeting.

Meeting Chairman: I'd also like to introduce Ramesh who recently joined our team.

Ramesh: May I also introduce my assistant, Sumit.

Meeting Chairman: Welcome Sumit.

Business Letter Writing: Writing a Cover Letter when Applying for a Job

The cover letter should always be included when sending your resume or CV for a possible job interview. This letter of application serves the purpose or introducing you and asking for an interview. Here is an outline to writing a successful cover letter. To the right of the letter, look for important notes concerning the layout of the letter signaled by a small number in red.

Cover Letter Outline

(Begin your cover letter by placing your address first, followed by the address of the company you are writing to.)

Lalit Upadhyay
D- 67, West End,
Dehradun

Mr. Bharat Bhushan,
Personnel Manager
(Use complete title and address; don't abbreviate.)
Arise Enterprises,
Industrial Area,
Patiala

Dear Mr. Bhushan,

(Always make an effort to write directly to the person in charge of hiring)

Opening paragraph — Use one of the following to bring yourself to the attention of the reader and make clear what job you are applying for:

Summarize the opening

Name the opening

Request an opening

Question the availability of an opening

Middle paragraph(s)- Use one of the following in each of your middle paragraphs to provide the reader with plenty of reasons to invite you to an interview:

Education

Work experience

Ability to work with others and/or alone

Interest in your field

Interest in the company

Responsibilities in previous positions

Closing paragraph - Use the closing paragraph to ensure action on the part of the reader

The last paragraph needs to help ensure that action is taken. You can ask for an interview appointment time, stating that you will be happy to come to the employer's office when convenient. Make it easy for the reader to follow-up by providing your telephone number and email address.

Sincerely,

Lalit Upadhyay
(Always sign letters.)
Enclosure

Some other basic business letters

Business Letter Writing: Sales Letters

The following letters introduce products for sales.

Useful Key Phrases

Are you having trouble ...

This is why it is important to have ...

At X, we have the skills and experience to ...

May we stop by and offer you a FREE estimate of how much it would cost to ...

If so, give us a call at X and set up and appointment with one of your friendly operators.

Example Letter

Document Makers
Sector- 5,
Gurgaon
March 10, 2008

Ravi Raj,
Senior Vice President,
New Sales Corporations

Dear Mr. Raj,

Are you having trouble getting your important documents formatted correctly? If you are like most business owners, you have trouble finding the time to economically produce good-looking documents. This is why it is important to have a specialist take care of your most important documents.

At Documents Makers, we have the skills and experience to come in and help you make the best possible impression. May we stop by and offer you a FREE estimate of how much it would cost to get your documents looking great? If so, give us a call at and set up and appointment with one of your friendly operators.

Sincerely,

(Sign here)
Pawan Kant
President

Business Letter Writing: Orders

The following letters place product orders.

Useful Key Phrases

Would you please send ...

According to your website / magazine / leaflet, ...

COD (cash on delivery)

NOTE: The initials at the bottom of the letter indicate who the letter is from followed by who typed the letter - for example: from Kavish Bansal typed by Rohit Malhotra = KB/rb

Business Letter Writing: Claim Letters

The following letters make claims against unsatisfactory work.

Useful Key Phrases

As someone who has worked with ...

we were very disappointed to find / see / have discovered ...

As our written agreement stipulated, we expected ...

I think you will agree that a communication problem exists.

We would like you to ..., or provide us with a refund.

Example Letter

Drivers Co.
34/89 Greene Avenue
Hyderabad
March 17, 2008

Ravi Singh
President
Document Makers
Sector- 5,
Gurgaon

Dear Mr. Singh,

As someone who has worked with your company for over three years, we were very disappointed to see the documents you produced for our latest Drivers Co. publicity campaign.

As our written agreement stipulated, we expected full color leaflets with fancy explanatory texts, but instead, we found that black and white photos had been included in the prepared leaflets. I think you will agree that a communication problem exists.

We would like you to send out a photographer to provide us with the promised color coverage, or provide us with a refund.

Yours Truly,

(Sign here)
Pankaj Jha,
Director

Business Letter Writing: Claim Adjustment Letters

The following letters adjust claims against unsatisfactory work.

Useful Key Phrases

I was very disappointed to read your letter of ... dealing with ...

As someone who values your business, I have already ...

Also, we will deduct another X percent of the bill for the misunderstanding.

Thank you for your patience.

Example Letter

Document Makers
Sector- 5,
Gurgaon
March 10, 2008

Pankaj Jha,
Director
Drivers Co.
34/89 Greene Avenue
Hyderabad

Dear Mr. Jha,

I was very disappointed to read your letter dealing with the issue of incorrectly produced publicity leaflets. As someone who values your business, I have already begun to find a solution to resolve this problem.

My top photographer will call you to arrange an appointment at your earliest possible convenience to re-take photos in full colour. Also, we will deduct another 15 percent of the bill for the misunderstanding. Thank you for your patience.

Sincerely,

(Sign here)
Ravi Singh
President

■

2

Acceptance, Acknowledgement and Announcement Letters

Acceptance of Counter Proposal

Dear Sidharth,

Your counter proposal on the project has been reviewed and is acceptable in its entirety.

We are enclosing an executed copy of the agreement along with two copies for your files. We are enthusiastically looking forward to this project and are pleased about having the opportunity to work together.

Yours Truly,

Ahan Sharma

Acceptance of Purchase Security Agreement

Dear Ramesh,

Attached is an accepted copy of your Purchase Security Agreement for the equipment.

There are three (3) remaining quarterly payments. Your first quarterly payment will be due on 2nd of next month, and we will mail you an invoice for it approximately one month prior to that date. Please return the remittance portion of the invoice with your cheque.

Under the Agreement, this contract is non-cancelable during the term of the contract. The balance, however, can be paid off at any time prior to the expiration of the contract.

We would like to take this opportunity to express our appreciation for your business. If you have any questions concerning your contract, or if we can be of service to you in any way, please let us know.

Yours Truly,

Sanjeev Seth (Head, Finance Department)

Acceptance of Resignation

Dear Saurabh,

It is with deep regret, that we accept your resignation as marketing executive of the our organisation.

We can appreciate the demands that this position has placed on you, and appreciate all of the fine contributions you have made as marketing executive.

Yours Truly,

Ramnaresh Agarwal (Head, Marketing)

Acknowledgement of Application

Date: 25th January, 2008

To,

Dinesh Singh

We appreciate your interest in being employed by our firm. We regret to inform you, however, that the available position has been filled, and we cannot give your application further consideration at the present time.

Your application will be kept on file for future reference should an opening arise.

Very Truly,

Raj Sharma (HR Head)

Acknowledgement of Cancellation of Backorder

Dear Ranbir,

We have received your letter acknowledging receipt of the items we mailed to you and noticing us to cancel shipment of your order for those items which are back ordered.

We will be issuing you a refund as soon as we have completed the necessary paperwork for your account.

We would like to take this opportunity to thank you for shopping through our new catalogue should be arriving at your home shortly, and I believe you will be pleased by some of the beautiful choices our buyers have made this season.

Thank you for your patience and understanding and for providing us with the opportunity to be of service to you.

Mandeep Singh

ABC Corporation

Acknowledgement of Change in Meeting Date

Dear Lalit,

Pursuant to your request, we have changed your meeting with Mr. Agarwal to 3.30 PM, on 24th of August.

We are pleased to be able to accommodate you in this manner, and Mr. Agarwal will be looking forward to your meeting on this newly appointed date.

Yours Truly,

Manoj Karnatak

Acknowledgement of Modified Terms

Date: 16th November, 2007

To: Shalabh Srivastava

Reference is made to the contract or order between us dated 14th October.

This letter will acknowledge that the contract is modified and superseded by some changes in terms.

Unless we immediately hear from you to the contrary, we shall assume said modification is mutually agreeable.

Very Truly,

Rakesh Jindal
XYZ Pvt. Ltd.

Acknowledgement of Request for Bid

Dear Alok,

Thank you for your request for bid on our project.

This letter is to acknowledge our receipt of said request and to advise you that we will be submitting our proposal on or before 15th September, 2008.

Rohit Seth

Project Head

Announcement of New Area Representative

Dear Abishek,

It is my great pleasure to advise you that Mr. Ravi Verma will now be representing our firm in your area.

Mr. Ravi Verma has been handling our accounts for some time and is extremely knowledgeable in this field.

Our new representative is scheduled to visit your office on 12th of September.

Yours Truly,

Anand Kumar

Announcement of New Area Representative Visit

Dear Suraj,

We have assigned Mr. Shalabh Srivastava as our new representative for your area. Mr. Shalabh Srivastava has been with our firm for quite some time and is extremely experienced in all aspects of our production.

Mr. Shalabh Srivastava will be coming to your city on 25th of August and will be calling on you in the morning if that doesn't conflict with your schedule. If there is any problem with that date, please let us know.

Jatin Singh

XYZ Sales Pvt. Ltd.

Announcement of New Business Opening

Gentlemen:

This is to inform you that Sun India ltd. is now open and is located at D-23, 4th Avenue, Bangalore.

Our store offers a complete and diverse line of computer software packages for both personal and business application. Since we do not represent any individual computer hardware manufacturer, the products that we carry are compatible with many systems. We are therefore able to offer to our customers a wide range of excellent software packages. Enclosed, for your review, is a partial list of the items we currently have available.

We hope that you will come and visit us soon.

Yours Truly,

Ravi John
Sun India Ltd.

Announcement of New Discount

Dear Sailja,

It is with great pleasure that we have recently welcomed Mr. Kapoor to our beauty salon. Mr. Kapoor was previously with another prestigious salon in Bangalore and we feel privileged that he has chosen to work with us.

We would like to take this opportunity to inform you of another change that has taken place in our salon. Now, if you make an appointment to have more than one treatment done on the same day, we are offering a discount. For example, if you are having your hair done and also having us apply sculptured nails, the cost for your nail application will be Rs. 25.00 instead of Rs. 30.00. The discount for a manicure or pedicure is Rs. 10.00 off our regular price.

We felt you would want to hear about this and are hoping to see you in the near future.

Latika Dhingra

Announcement of Free Delivery Limitations Change

Dear Somesh,

There has been a change in our delivery service policy which we would like to bring to your attention.

We have always provided free delivery for any orders placed with the firm, regardless of the size of the order. Due to the increase in the price of fuel, we must now limit this free delivery service to any orders over Rs. 1000. We regret the necessity of imposing this restriction.

We wish to take this opportunity to thank you for being one of our most valued customers.

Yours Truly,

Ravi Singh

Announcement of New Pricing Policy

Gentlemen

It has been our policy in the past to supply ice to our customers when their ice machine has broken down. Because we have many customers who are paying later and later, we are forced to set down stronger company policies. Our new policy will go into effect from August 3, 2008, and is as follows:

1. If the customer is more than 15 days late in their monthly payment and the machine is not working, we will not supply ice. We will repair the machine, and the number of days in which the machine has not been in service will be credited to the customer's account. At the time of our service call we will expect payment in full of any unpaid balance due us.
2. There will be a surcharge on accounts falling more than 30 days behind.

While I am sorry that we must go to such extremes as those outlined above, I am afraid that there is no alternative. Our company policy is, and always has been, to provide the best service available to our customers. We can only continue to do this with our customer's cooperation.

If there are any questions regarding our new policy, please give me a call.

Aditya Sehgal

XYZ India Ltd.

Announcement of Partnership Buyout

Gentlemen

This is to inform you that I have purchased all of the interest of my former partner, Ashish, and that he is no longer associated with the firm.

Our business will continue to provide the same high quality products and service on which we have built our reputation and this internal change will in no way effect our company policy or manner of conducting business.

I would like to take this opportunity to thank you for the courtesies you have shown us in the past, and hope that you will let us continue to serve your business in a way that is mutually beneficial and profitable to us both.

Santosh Singh

ABC Sales

Announcement of Price Increase

Dear Karthik,

Due to the increase in raw material costs, we must unfortunately raise the cost of our merchandise to you.

We have avoided raising our prices for as long as possible, but we can no longer prolong the inevitable. We have enclosed our new price list for your review which goes into effect from 22nd of September. Any orders placed between now and 22nd of September will be honored at the lower prices.

We wish to thank you for your valued account and know that you will understand the necessity for this price increase.

Rohan Mathur

■

3

Apology Letters

Apology after Cancellation of Order

Dear Manoj,

This is to acknowledge receipt of your letter of 6th March, 2008 in which you set forth your reasons for canceling your purchase order.

I am very sorry about the misunderstanding that led to this cancellation and has taken the matter up with management in order to ensure that a problem of this nature does not occur again.

As one of our valued customers, your satisfaction is one of our primary concerns. Please accept our apology.

Yours Truly,

Ravikant Singh

Apology and Replacement of Damaged Goods

Dear Lalit,

It was distressing to learn that the chocolate we shipped to your firm last week arrived in bits and pieces. Per your request, a new shipment left our dock this morning and is scheduled for afternoon delivery to you on October 26th. Please turn over the damaged goods to the driver at the time of deliver.

I am sorry that this unfortunate incident occurred and sincerely appreciate your continued patronage.

Yours Truly,

Rajesh Jain

Apology and Request for Extension of Time to Deliver Goods

Dear Rajat,

This is to acknowledge that we are in receipt of your notice whereby you informed us that the goods shipped to you on 2nd February, 2008 did not conform to our agreement dated 3rd January 2008.

We regret this unintentional mistake on our part. While we recognize that the time for performing under this agreement has expired, we are requesting that you extend the time to 1st May in order that we may cure the defect by replacing the shipment with goods that conform to our agreement.

Please accept our apology for this inconvenience. We will be looking forward to your response.

Yours Truly,

Tushar Kant

Apology for Delay of Refund

Dear Ravi,

After reading your letter of 8th June, I can thoroughly understand why you are running out of patience.

While it would be easy to place the blame on our computer, this poor fellow has received enough abuse since joining our firm. After all, he only follows the orders that are given to him.

Therefore, please accept my apology for the delay in refunding your money. Our bookkeeping department has been instructed to issue a cheque to you at once, which you should be receiving within a few days. I am grateful that your letter was brought to my attention and I appreciate your perseverance in settling this matter. Once again, I am very sorry for the inconvenience this has caused you.

Yours,

Meghua Lal

Apology for Delayed Response & Request for Meeting

Gentlemen:

This is to inform you that we are unable to make delivery on the above referenced purchase order on the date indicated.

We should have our merchandise ready to ship within 10 days of the original delivery date and we hope that you can hold off until that time.

We did want to inform you of this delay as soon we were advised in order to give you as much time as possible to make alternate arrangements, if necessary. We can assure you, however, that if your order remains in force we will expedite delivery to you as soon as we have received the merchandise.

Please accept our apology for this delay and thank you for your understanding.

Yours,

Deepak Kumar

Apology for Poor Service Rating on Customer Questionnaire

Dear Kavita,

Thank you for taking the time to fill out our questionnaire during your stay with us. We do appreciate hearing from our customers, as their comments are vital for us to continue improving our accommodations.

The problems that you mentioned have been brought to the attention of our housekeeping department. While the lack of service you experienced is unusual and not the standard of our motel, there is no excuse for a lackadaisical attitude on the part of any of our employees. We are sorry for the inconvenience and annoyance this incident caused.

Thank you again for your comments. We hope that you will give us another chance to serve you.

Yours Truly,

Aditi Dayal

Friendly Apology for Late Payment

Dear Rohan,

Your letter arrived a few days ago and I must confess that this obligation completely slipped my mind. Needless to say, there is no excuse for this and I extend my sincerest apologies along with the attached cheque.

Please accept our warmest regards and sincerest hope that all is well. We certainly look forward to meeting you in the near future.

Again, thank you for the hospitality you extended to our son during the vacation period. I am sure Rob has enjoyed and will continue to enjoy the friendship of your son.

Yours,

Ravish Kishen

Apology & Proposal on Overshipped Merchandise

Dear Jacob,

In deference to your valuable time, I would like to get straight to the point and say that we were wrong.

Your purchase order clearly stated 30 cases. The shipment of 60 cases was our error.

Meanwhile, there are two options available at this time; you can keep the additional merchandise and we will bill you thirty days from now, or we will arrange to have it picked up at your loading dock and issue a credit to you. Please let me know of your preference.

We will do everything in our power to ensure that this type of error does not occur again. Thank you for your understanding. If I can be of any assistance in any way, please do not hesitate to call on me.

Yours Truly,

Lalit Singhal

Apology and Tender of Compensation

Dear Girish,

Thank you for your letter of 2nd August, you informed us that product you purchased was defected and not working properly.

We are sorry that you experienced this problem and are enclosing compensation for this. While we make every attempt to ensure that our products are safe, this unfortunate incident can occasionally occur.

We are very appreciative that you have taken the time to bring this to our attention and would like to thank you for purchasing our products.

Yours Truly,

Pawan Kumar

Apology for Accounting Errors and Past Due Notices

Dear Akash,

You deserve an explanation for what went wrong in our accounting department, and I hope that this letter will serve to resolve our recent difficulties.

I know that you can appreciate the fact that it has taken some time to find out exactly what occurred, and, therefore, please accept our apologies for the delay in this response.

Apparently, your payment was received in a timely fashion, but it was credited to an account which bears a similar name to yours. Therefore, we commenced sending you our standard notices requesting payment, in keeping with our routine policy. Even after the posting error was rectified, our accounting department failed to notify our credit department, which is why you continued to receive our correspondence demanding payment.

I know how exasperating this has been for you and I am deeply sorry that it has taken so long to straighten out this problem. While there is a procedure within our firm to preclude this type of error from occurring, we are reinforcing this procedure.

You have been a valued customer of ours for a long time and we appreciate your affording us the opportunity to serve you. You may rest assured that this problem will not surface again.

Yours Truly,

Manohar Kumar

Apology for Not Crediting Payment

Dear Ranjan,

Thank you for your assistance in helping us to locate your payment of 11th February, which had not been credited to your account.

Please accept our apology for this error and for the overdue notices we sent to you.

We appreciate your patronage and are sorry for the inconvenience caused by this error.

Ravi Verma

Accounts Head

Apology for Not Crediting Payment from Prompt Payer

Dear Kamal,

Thank you for your letter and the photocopy of your cheque, which showed that your account had been paid in full. While we are very sorry for the inconvenience this has caused you, the enclosure of your cheque enabled us to go through our records and pinpoint how this error occurred.

Please accept our apology for the letters we wrote under the assumption that this bill had not been paid. I know this insistence on our part must have been extremely frustrating for you, especially in light of the fact that you have always been a valued customer of ours and have paid your bills promptly.

Thank you for your patience and please be assured that we will do everything in our power to ensure that this type of error does not occur in the future.

Yours Truly,

Manoj Joshi

Apology to Receiver of NSF Cheque

Dear Santosh,

When I received your letter of May 3, with my cheque attached marked "insufficient funds", I called my bank immediately.

The gentleman I spoke with, discovered that the bank had failed to credit my account with a substantial deposit I had made several days prior.

The bank has assured me that they will be sending you a formal letter of apology for their error. Attached is my cheque in the amount of Rs. 50,000 to replace the dishonoured one you have returned.

Yours Truly,

Aditya Sharma

■

4

Congratulations Letters

Congratulations on Expansion

Dear Ravi,

When we received your notice of expansion, we at Global Systems were elated.

There are few firms that can boast of the success you have achieved over such a relatively short period of time. A great deal of that success, in our opinion, must be directly attributed to your strong leadership and the sense of direction that you provide.

Please accept our heartiest congratulations and best wishes for your continued success.

Yours Truly,

Manoj Karnatak

Congratulations on Formation of New Company

Dear Santosh,

It was with great pleasure that I read your announcement of the formation of your new company. You have certainly chosen an area that is coming into its own. I know that with your background, expertise and enthusiasm, your firm should make quite an impression in the industry.

My congratulations and best wishes for your success.

Yours Truly,

Manohar Kumar

Congratulations on Increased Sales

To: Sales Deparment Members

Subject: Monthly Results

The numbers are in and I am proud to inform you that our total sales for the period of April 15th through May 15th amount to over Rs. 50 Lakh, which represents a 20% increase over our sales for the preceding period.

You have achieved the goal we established in the first week of April, and you are all to be highly commended for your achievement. Congratulations!

Deepesh Kumar

Sales Head

Congratulations on Outstanding Achievement

Dear Krishna,

You have proven the skeptics wrong and accomplished what most said was impossible.

There is no doubt that your recent achievements will be spoken of for some time to come and that the admiration for your accomplishments is felt by all of us within the industry as well as the general public.

Please accept my heartiest congratulations for your success.

Yours Truly,

Sanjay Sharma

Congratulations to New Business

Dear Sahil,

Congratulations on the opening of your new gallery.

We know that every business requires a good bookkeeping system, and have developed complete programmes for businesses of all sizes. While some systems are more extensive than others, they all have a mutual goal; to minimize paperwork, conserve time spent on bookkeeping, and provide a simple format for keeping records in good order.

I have enclosed our brochure and price list for your review. Upon your request, I will be happy to arrange a convenient time for one of our salesmen to meet with you at your location.

Best wishes for your success.

Yours,

Lalit Singhal

Congratulations to New Owners

Dear Mukul,

As the new owners of the company, please accept our congratulations and very best wishes for your success.

DC Fresh is a well established supplier of meat and provisions to many of the finer hotels and restaurants in the city and its vicinity. We specialize in different categories of meat. We have enclosed a price list for your review, but would like to add that there are specific quantity discounts that are available.

Mr. Shyamal Das, our sales representative for your area would be pleased to come to meet you at your convenience to show you the quality of our products and discuss our terms and prices with you. Please call for an appointment.

Dinesh Upadhyay

DC Fresh Ltd.

Congratulations on a Job Well Done

Dear Kavita,

The displays you created for the "Summer's Coming" promotion are just beautiful. Several of the sales personnel told me that they have received numerous compliments from the customers.

Congratulations on a job well done.

Kritika Desai

Sales Head

Congratulations to Employee on 5-Years Anniversary

Dear Akash,

October 21st will mark your fifth anniversary as a member of our firm. We would like to take this opportunity to thank you for these past five years of fine workmanship and company loyalty.

We know that the growth and success of our company is largely dependent on having strong and capable staff members, such as yourself, and recognize the contribution you make in helping us maintain the position we enjoy in the industry.

We are hoping that you will remain with us for many years to come and would like to offer our congratulations on this anniversary.

Pawan Kumar

HR Department

■

5

Demand and Denial Letters

Denial of Request for Additional Discount

Dear Vijay,

This letter is in response to your inquiry regarding our flexibility in the discount rate we offer for early settlement of accounts.

Our established discount is 2% of the total invoiced amount when payment is received within 10 days of delivery. This figure is not one that has been arbitrarily chosen, but is based on cost, overhead and profit. To increase this discount rate for all of our accounts would seriously jeopardise our firm and to increase the rate for an individual account would be both unfair and unethical.

I believe that you will find that the 2% discount rate we offer our customers is standard in the industry.

We consider you a most valued customer and hope that you can appreciate our position in this matter. If we are able to accommodate you in any way that is within our company policy, we will be most happy to do so.

Very Truly,

Raviraj Sharma

Demand to Endorsers for Immediate Payment

Date: 24th of May, 2008

To: Kailash Kumar

The undersigned is the holder of the cheque to which you are an endorser.

Notice is hereby provided that said instrument has not been paid, and protest and demand is hereby made upon you to immediately pay the face amount of the instrument in the amount of Rs. 50,000. In the event payment is not made within five (5) days, the undersigned shall proceed to suit on your warranties of endorsement.

Manohar Kant

Demand by Secured Party for Possession of Collateral

Date: 12th of January, 2008

To: Naman Ahuja (debtor)

This is to advise you that you are in default under our security agreement dated 4th of February, 2004.

Accordingly, I demand that you surrender possession of the collateral to me at once as provided in the security agreement and Uniform Commercial Code.

Very Truly,

Saurabh Sharma
(Secured Party)

Demand for Acknowledgement of Shipping Dates

Date: 12th of February, 2008

To: ABC Suppliers

We hereby request that you specify shipping arrangements pursuant to our order and that you furnish us assurance that you shall comply. Default in seasonable and sufficient assurance from you shall constitute a breach of said contract and we shall no longer be obligated under said contract.

Very Truly,

Gulab Kumar

Demand on Guarantor

Date: 16th of November, 2007

To: Narayan Kumar

The undersigned is the holder of your guarantee wherein you guarantee the debt owed us. Please be advised that payments on said debt are in default. Accordingly, demand is made upon you as a guarantor to fully pay the outstanding debt due us in the amount of Rs 1,000,000.

Very Truly,

Pawan Kumar

Denial of Request for Extension of Time

Dear Sandhya,

This is to acknowledge receipt of your letter of 21st of August, in which you requested a three month extension on your loan.

After careful review, we regret to inform you that we are unable to grant you any further extensions for the payment on your loan.

We are sorry about the difficulties you are experiencing, but we must insist on receiving your payment by due date.

We hope that you will be able to find another solution to your problem.

Yours Truly,

Parkash Gurani

Decline to Interview Referred Job Applicant

Dear Rohit,

Having been away from the office for a few days, I didn't read your letter of May 19th until today.

While I am sure the young man you wrote to me about wouldn't warrant the recommendation you gave unless he is truly exceptional, I believe it would be unfair to him to set up an interview at this time. We have just had to lay off twenty four employees and there is no way that I could justify hiring someone new under those circumstances. We anticipate that business should improve over the next six months, but for now, the timing is off.

I am sorry to have to disappoint you. You know, under the right circumstances, we are always looking for bright young people with potential.

Thank you for thinking of us.

Your faithfully

Gopal Pant

■

(6)

Employer and Employee Related Letters

Employee Invention Agreement

For good considerations, and in consideration of the undersigned being employed by our company; the undersigned hereby agrees, acknowledges and represents:

1. The undersigned, during the course of employment, shall promptly disclose in writing to the company all inventions, discoveries, improvements, developments and innovations whether patentable or not, conceived in whole or in part by the undersigned or through assistance of the undersigned, and whether conceived or developed during working hours or not, which:
   a) Result from any work performed on behalf of Company, or pursuant to a suggested research project by the Company, or
   b) Relate in any manner to the existing or contemplated business of the Company, or
   c) Result from the use of the Company's time, material, employees or facilities.
2. The undersigned hereby assigns to the Company, its successors and assigns, all right, title and interest to said inventions.
3. The undersigned shall, at the Company's request, execute specific assignments to any such invention and execute, acknowledge, and deliver any additional documents required to obtain letters patent in any jurisdiction and shall, at the Company's request and expense, assist in the defense and prosecution of said letters patent as may be required by Company. This provision shall survive termination of employ with the Company.

Signed under seal this Monday, 25th of November. 2005.

Prashant Raj

(Employee)

Employee Non-Compete Agreement

For good considerations, and in consideration of my being employed by this company, I, the undersigned, hereby agree that upon my termination of employment and notwithstanding the cause of termination, I shall not compete with the business of the Company, or its successors or assigns.

The term "not compete" as used in this agreement means that I shall not directly or indirectly own, be employed by or work on behalf of any firm engaged in a business substantially similar and competitive with the Company.

This non-compete agreement shall remain in full force and effect for 3 years commencing with the date of employment termination.

Signed under seal this Monday, 25th of November, 2007.

Avinash Kumar

(Employee)

Employee Suggestion for Company Meeting

Dear Ashutosh,

There is such a high degree of anxiety about the proposed merger with another firm that I can see the effects in my department daily. I do not feel that the newsletter put out last week helped assuage the fears of the other employees.

I believe that it might be beneficial to meet the issue head-on by holding a meeting wherein questions can be put forth and answers can be provided. There is a schism between employees and management that appears to be growing and presents a potential problem. If, for example, this merger fails to materialize, the employees may maintain their current feelings of alienation to the detriment of the organisation.

I know that there are many inherent problems in hashing this subject out in an open forum and these must be weighed against the present alternative. I do feel, however, that the suggestion is worth some consideration.

Very Truly,

Kapil Vats

Employment Reimbursement Agreement

The undersigned officer or employee of this company, agrees to repay to the Company all compensation payments or reimbursements that are disallowed, in whole or in part, as a deductible expense by the Internal Revenue Service.

The reimbursement shall be made to the full extent of the disallowance upon an adverse decision of the last tribunal or agency to consider the issue, provided the Company shall not be obligated to seek further appeal if available.

Signed under seal this Monday, 25th of November, 2008.

Pradeep Mahajan

(Employee)

Employment Letter

Date: 12th of January, 2008

Dear Aman,

We are pleased to confirm your being employed by our firm in the capacity of senior accountant. You will report directly to accounts manager, commencing with your start of employment on 13th of January, 2008.

Your salary shall be Rs 15,000 per month. You will also be covered by the standard group benefit plans and fringe benefits explained to you. For the first year vacation time shall be pro-rated, so you will be entitled to 15 days vacation for this year. If you agree, this letter sets for the our understanding, please sign the enclosed copy and return for our files. We look forward to your joining the company.

Very Truly,

Peter Michaels
HR Head

Complimentary Letter to Employee on Handling of Difficult Situation

Dear Ishant,

Several of your associates in the shipping department have informed me of the incident that occurred last Friday with a representative of ABC Supplies. They have all agreed that this driver hurled some extremely abusive language at you and that his actions were unjustifiably offensive.

They also all agreed that you remained a gentleman throughout the entire time, attempting to solve the problem. I compliment you on your self-control, and in handling the situation in such an exemplary manner. I have placed a call to the owner of Gene's Tools and fully anticipate your receiving an apology from them.

Yours Truly,

Avinash Singh
Senior Manager

Complimentary Letter to Employee on Handling of an Emergency

Dear Tarun,

You are to be highly commended for the way you handled the emergency that occurred yesterday. The paramedics have informed us that if you hadn't acted as quickly as you did, our customer's attack might have been fatal.

Thanks to your fast reaction, she is already out of intensive care and on the road to recovery. We are very proud of your association with our organisation.

Yours Truly,

Rasik Sahay

Employment Agreement

Agreement made between ABC Corporations, herein referred to as "Company", and Mr. Deepak Sehgal, herein referred to as "Employee".

Company hereby employs employee to perform such duties at such times and in such manner as the company may from time to time direct. Employee agrees that he will perform those duties assigned to him to the best of his ability, to maintain a current and complete account of his work and expenses, to remit promptly to the company any monies paid to him or coming into his possession which belong to the company, to devote his full and undivided time to the transaction of company business and to refrain from being engaged in any other business during the tenure of his employment with the company. In consideration of the foregoing, company agrees to pay to employee the amount of Rs. 20,000 for a period of three months, plus reasonable travel expenses incurred for the purpose of conducting company business.

This contract shall become effective on 1st of march and remain in effect until it is terminated by either party. Either party may terminate this agreement by providing the other party with 30 day's written notice of his or their intention.

Should this agreement be terminated by either party, employee agrees that the payment in full to the date of termination shall fully satisfy all claims against the company under this agreement.

Rajat Kapoor

(Signatures)

(for ABC Corporations)

and Aman Seth

(employee)

■

7

Explanation and Legal Letters

Explanation for Delay of Partial Shipment

Dear Rakesh,

After some investigation, I believe that we have found the source of the problem that led us to our misunderstanding on 14th of May.

When we received your purchase order for the product, we were unable to fill the order for immediate delivery due to some technical reasons.

Our letter informing you of this delay and requesting your instructions was mailed to you on 16th of April. We did not receive a reply and proceeded to send a follow-up letter to you on 26th of April.

We have been able to make delivery to you since then but felt that since you had emphasized "for immediate delivery" on your purchase order, we should wait for your authorisation before shipping.

I can easily understand why you were so upset with us if no one made you aware of our correspondence. We have always appreciated having you as a customer and hope that we can continue to provide you with our products in the future.

Yours Truly,

Mahesh Singhal

Explanation of Insurance Rate Increase

Dear Sharad,

We are in receipt of a directive from XYZ Sales concerning the above captioned Regulation. This new regulation went into effect on 1st of February and requires that complications of pregnancy be covered in the same manner as any other injury or disease.

"Complications" is defined as anything other than a normal delivery. This is applicable to any employee, dependent spouse or dependent child.

Due to the potential increase in claims, it has become necessary to increase our quoted rates to comply with this regulation.

If you have any questions regarding these rate increases due to the change in regulations, please feel free to call.

Sharad Saxena

Final Notice Before Legal Action

Date: 12th of September, 2007

To: Lalit Seth

We have repeatedly requested payment of Rs. 50,000 on your overdue account. Our demands for payment have been ignored.

Accordingly, we shall turn this account over for collection within the next ten days unless payment, or an acceptable proposal for payment is obtained. Enforced collection on this obligation may result in additional legal or court costs to you and may impair your credit rating.

Very Truly,

K. Thomas

Overdue Payment Reminder, Notice of Credit Hold

Dear Akash,

It is because we do not want you to experience unnecessary embarrassment, that we are writing this letter to you.

As we have reminded you, your account is past due and I am sorry to inform you that if you were to present your charge card at our store today, our sales personnel could not accept the charge without an okay from the credit department. This would necessitate your going to the credit department to discuss the status of your bill before the charge would be approved.

You have been too good of a customer in the past to have to go through this procedure, but unless we receive your payment we have no other alternative, due to our company policy. We have enclosed a self-addressed envelope for your convenience and are requesting that you please mail us your payment today. Thank you for your anticipated cooperation.

Yours Truly,

Sidharth Seth

Final Warning before Dismissal

Date: 21st of October, 2007

To: Santosh Singhal

You have been previously notified of certain problems in your performance as an employee, which problems appear to continue.

Any further violations of company policy or failure to perform in accordance with our standards shall result in immediate dismissal without further warning.

Deepak Kapoor

Letter Notice of Litigation

Dear Lalit,

All of our efforts to settle the above matter amicably have been unsuccessful. We have made numerous calls and, to date, have not had the courtesy of a call back. We have delayed legal proceedings up to now based on your assurances that we would be paid in full by 23rd of July. I am enclosing copies of your letters stating that intention.

Please be advised that you have left us no alternative but to file suit immediately. We have attempted to be understanding of your cash flow problems but our patience has now reached an end.

Your account is being turned over to our attorney. While I regret the necessity of this action I must advise you to govern yourself accordingly.

Yours Truly,

Kapil Kumar

Final Demand for Payment on Delinquent Account

Dear Manoj,

Your account has been referred to me with instructions that I make final demand for payment of this debt.

In as much as the outstanding balance is sizable, I have outlined a payment plan for you as a method to retire the entire balance over the next 3 months if you are unable to forward the full amount at this time.

Amount Due Rs 80,000

Due Date 12th of May, 2005

This offer is being made to you as our expression of wanting to settle your account in an amicable manner. If we do not receive your first payment by the date indicated above, we will have no choice but to refer your account to a collection agency. We do not wish to take any action which might impair your credit rating and therefore request that you give this matter your most immediate attention.

Yours Truly,

Deepak Kapoor
(Accounts Head)

Final Notice of Impending Litigation

Dear Saurabh,

The postmark of this letter is registered with our office. Unless you contact us, you will run the risk of your local lawyer serving you with a Summons and Complaint to appear in Court without further notice to you.

Filing of suit will initiate a series of events that will cause you considerable inconvenience and expense. In addition to the above mentioned balance, you may be liable for court costs and interest. In the event you should fail to contact us immediately, we will assume that this debt is valid. Should you have any reason to dispute the validity of the debt or any portion thereof, this office will obtain verification of the debt or obtain a copy of the judgement and mail you a copy of same. This office will also provide you with the name and address of the original creditor if different from the current creditor. Please govern yourself accordingly.

Yours Truly,

Ravi Mohan

■

(8)

Notice Letters

Notice and Tender by Debtor

To: Naresh Kumar

You are hereby notified that the undersigned elects to redeem the collateral that is currently in your possession pursuant to that certain security agreement, for which said collateral was pledged to secure performance.

Therefore, the undersigned hereby tenders fulfillment of all obligations pursuant to said security agreement and secured by said collateral, in addition to the amount of Rs. 1,00,000 for your expenses in repossessing, holding, preparing the collateral for disposition through sale, arranging for sale, attorney's fees and legal expenses. Demand is hereby made that you make the said collateral available for retaking by the undersigned.

(Signature)

Kamal Kumar

Notice of Cancellation of Contract

To: ABC Sales Pvt. Ltd.

Notice is hereby given that we cancel our contract dated 14th of March, 2008 for the sale of some goods to ABC Sales Pvt. Ltd., for some reasons.

Cancellation of said contract is effected in respect to that certain installment delivered on 15th of April, and for any subsequent delivery of goods, contracted for in said contract, in as much as your breach impairs the contract as a whole.

(We claim damages from you in the amount of Rs. 50,000)

Dated 21st of April, 2008

(Signature)

Deepak Kapoor
(For City Corporations)

Notice of Annual Meeting of Shareholders

ABC Corporations

Dear Shareholder,

Notice is hereby given that the annual meeting of the shareholders of ABC Corporations will be held at the company's headquarters in Mumbai on 21st of September, 2008, at 11 AM. The new business of the company will be discussed at the meeting.

In the event that you will be unable to attend this annual meeting, we are requesting that you execute and mail the enclosed form of proxy to the secretary of our company so that your shares may be regularly voted at the meeting.

(Signature)

Anant Thakur
(For ABC Corporations)

Notice of Change of Address

Dear Manoj,

As of Monday, October 1, 2008, Arise Sales Corporation of India's Eastern Regional Office will be located in our new offices and warehouse building at 12/5, Chowranghi Lane, Calcutta. The telephone number for this new location is (033) 25505428. Our Manufacturing Division will remain at the old address. I have enclosed our most recent brochure on robotic equipment for your review. I hope you find it interesting.

Yours Truly,

Ramesh Sahay (Arise Sales Corporation of India)

Notice of Defective Goods

Date: 23rd of September, 2007

To: City Corporations

We are in receipt of merchandise shipped to us pursuant to your invoice, dated 4th of September, 2007. Certain goods as listed on the attached sheet are defective for the some reasons.

Accordingly, we reject said defective goods, demand credit or adjustment and intend to re-ship said goods to you at your expense. Please confirm credit issue and issue instructions for return of defective goods.

Very Truly,

Arvind Jain
Arise Sales Corporation

Notice of Impending Litigation After Unproductive Arrangements

Dear Kunal,

Productivity is an important guideline in any business. When we find that our productivity suffers we naturally become concerned. Well, we are concerned about our productivity in collecting the amount owed on your account.

We have invested much time in attempting to work out arrangements for the payment of your account and it seems that each agreement is met with a lack of productivity. Therefore, we must insist that payment be received within ten days of this notice. Otherwise, we will have no alternative other than to forward your account to our attorney.

Yours Truly,

Satish Kumar

Notice of Delayed Shipment

Dear Amit,

Due to the huge response we received from our summer catalogue, we are experiencing a delay in filling some of the orders. Items you ordered should be sent to you within 3 weeks from this date of 12th of January, 2008.

Please accept our apologies for this delay.

Yours Truly,

Ganesh Pathak

Notice of Dishonoured Cheque

Date: 2nd of April, 2008

To: Sumit Singh

Your cheque of Rs. 50,000, tendered to us on 25th of March, 2008 has been dishonoured by your bank. Unless we receive good funds for said amount within 10 days of receipt of this notice, we shall have no alternative but to commence appropriate legal action for its recovery.

Very Truly,

Dhiraj Kumar

Notice of Inability to Ship

Dear Prashant,

Due to the fire we sustained on 4th of March, 2007 , we regret to inform you that we will be unable to ship the merchandise for your purchase order as scheduled.

We do anticipate our production resuming on 10th of April, and will be able to fill orders then.

Thank you for your understanding.

Yours Truly,

Naresh Kumar

Notice of Intention to Make a Private Sale After Breach

Gentlemen:

Due to the fact that we have not received your payment for the goods we have delivered to you in accordance with our contract entered into on 21st of January, 2008 , and that in failing to pay for these goods you are in breach of said contract, as you were noticed, it is our intention to make a private sale of the goods which we have manufactured for the balance of goods to be delivered under that certain contract, but which are undeliverable due to said breach, for a purchase price of Rs. 10,0,000.

This sale is to be consummated on 3rd of March, 2008 and will go forward if your default is not cured.

It is our desire to inform you of the foregoing and afford you the opportunity to decide on a course of action, in view of the fact that you will be held liable for the loss sustained by us on said resale to the extent authorized by the law.

Yours Truly,

Vivek Singh

Notice of Intention to Sell Goods After Breach

Dear Mamta,

When we were notified of your breach of contract, there were several units of goods being manufactured in our plant, which were intended for delivery to you under the contract we entered on 21st of September, 2007.

It is commercially unreasonable for us to proceed to complete these units, and are therefore notifying you of our intent to offer these unfinished units for sale in the near future. We will, of course, be sending you a notice when a specific time and date has been set for said sale.

Although we are under no obligation, we are providing you with you with this advanced notice as to our intentions in this matter.

Yours Truly,

Charu Mathur

Notice of Non-Conforming Goods

Date: 21st of September, 2007

To: ABC Sales

We are in receipt of certain goods recently shipped to us under the attached invoices.

Certain goods as shipped do not conform to specification or sample in some of the particulars attached separately. Accordingly, we hereby reject said non-conforming goods and demand issue of credit and instructions for return at your expense.

Very Truly,

Manoj Kumar

Notice of Private Sale of Collateral

Date: 1st of September, 2007

To: Kunal Kapoor

You are hereby notified that after 22nd of September, 2007, the undersigned shall sell at private sale the collateral.

Said collateral shall be sold to any buyer for the amount of Rs. 2,00,000.

You will be held liable for any deficiency resulting from said sale.

You may redeem this property by paying the amount due and accrued costs of foreclosure at any time prior to the time of sale.

Very Truly,

Ramesh Talwar
(Secured Party)

Notice of Promotion

Dear Ayush,

It is our great pleasure to inform you that you have been promoted to the challenging and demanding position of team leader in the marketing department.

This promotion is in recognition of the fine work you have done for this firm. We are very confident that you will meet the new responsibilities which accompany the position of team leader with the same level of enthusiasm and enterprise which you have exhibited since you came to work with our firm.

Please accept our congratulations on your new promotion.

Mahesh Thakur

Marketing Head

Notice of Public Sale of Collateral

Date: 23rd of February, 2009

To: Dinesh Singh

You are hereby given notice that the collateral covered under our security agreement shall be sold at public auction on 25th of March, 2009. Time and location for that auction is described under.

Time: 11 AM onwards Location: City Centre

You will be held liable for any deficiency resulting from said sale.

You may redeem this property by paying the amount due and accrued costs of foreclosure at any time prior to the time of sale.

Very Truly,

Ravi Singh
(Secured Party)

Notice of Rejected Bid

Dear Sunder,

Thank you very much for the proposal you submitted to us in response to our request.

We are aware of the great deal of time and work that went into your bid and therefore, regret to inform you that we have awarded the contract to another firm. We based our decision on certain undisclosed terms.

We will certainly be inviting your firm to bid on our future projects and thank you once again for your proposal.

Yours Truly,

Om Mathur

Notice of Refusal to Accept Delivery

Date: 23rd of February, 2008

To: Ravikant Saini

We are in receipt of your order described on the attached invoice or order form. You have cancelled the order after acceptance or refused to accept delivery.

Accordingly, we consider our obligations to attempt further shipment as terminated, reserving all rights against you for resultant damages arising from your failure to fulfill your obligations.

Very Truly,

Lalit Singh

Notice of Withheld Delivery

Date: 16th of May, 2008

To: Lalit Joshi

Reference is made to your order for certain goods under date of 12th of March, 2008, we are withholding delivery for the reason(s) checked:

- Required payment has not been made.
- You repudiated or withdrew your contract to buy.
- You failed to furnish requested shipping instructions.
- Certain goods are back ordered and shipment will be made in single lot.

Very Truly,

Amit Mishra

Notice of Reclamation

Date: 23rd of February, 2008

To: Amitabh Saxena

Certain goods have been shipped to you within the past ten days as represented by the attached invoices. It has come to our attention that your firm is insolvent, and therefore we demand return and reclamation of all goods delivered to you within the ten days preceding this notice.

Very Truly,

Pawan Kumar

Notice of Rejected Counter-Proposal

Dear Rohit,

After spending a considerable amount of time going over your counter proposal, my associates and I concluded that the terms are simply unworkable, and, from our point of view, unrealistic.

If you wish to reconsider our original proposal please let me know.

Yours,

Neeru Kansal

Notice on Receipt of Un-acceptable Merchandise

Dear Arnav,

This is to acknowledge receipt of the order and to inform you that the merchandise does not meet my specifications.

Whereas I ordered is not the same what you sent me. In as much as this item was intended as a gift, I must cancel my order and request a refund for the merchandise.

If you will provide me with your instructions for returning this merchandise to your firm, I will arrange for its speedy delivery.

Yours Truly,

Anand Jain

Notice of Return of Goods Sold on Approval

Date: 23rd of February, 2008

To: ABC Suppliers

The undersigned hereby returns to you the goods purchased from you on approval on 14th of January, 2008; said goods consisting of many problems.

Very Truly,

Askok Rai

Notice of Un-satisfactory Performance

Date: 16th of May, 2008

To: Prashant Singh

Confirming our meeting relative to certain unsatisfactory aspects of your performance, we expect that in the future you shall improve your performance.

We have every confidence the problem will not be repeated.

Yours,

Sudhir Joshi

Notice to Cancel Entire Order

Date: 4th of June, 2008

To: XYZ Pvt. Ltd.

Reference is made to our purchase order or contract dated 3rd of September, 2007, a copy of which is enclosed.

Due to your failure to ship the goods within the time required, we hereby cancel said order, reserving such further rights we may have.

Very Truly,

Rakesh Anand

Notice to Cancel Shipment of Back-Ordered Goods

Date: 16th of May, 2008

To: City Corporations

Reference is made to our purchase order or contract dated 4th of April, a copy of which is attached.

We have received a partial shipment and notice that certain goods are out of stock or on back order.

Please cancel our order for the back-ordered goods and adjust our invoice for goods received.

Very Truly,

Sidharth Roy

Notice to Deliver Possession

Dear Radha,

Reference is made to your Lease dated 5th of November, 2005, by and between lessor and lessee, for a month-to-month term.

You are hereby notified to deliver up possession of the hereinafter described premises you now hold in possession, on a month-to month tenancy, within days from the date indicated above. Said premises known as arise house, located at 3rd street, mahatma Gandhi road, Bangalore, to be surrendered to the Landlord.

Thank you for your cooperation in this matter.

Yours Truly,

Vijay Pratap

Notice to Employees of New Vacation Policy

To: All Employees
From: Management

Subject: Vacations

This is to provide a notice to all employees of our new company policy in regards to vacations.

Notice of your intention to take a vacation must be given to the company no less than 15 days prior to your vacation.

This will enable us to employ temporary help, if necessary, and to schedule vacations in a manner that will not be disruptive to the company.

Thank you for your cooperation.

Notice to Pay Rent or Quit

To: Tenant in possession

You are hereby required to pay the rent on the premises herein described, of which you now hold possession, pursuant to a written lease, amounting to Rs. 1,00,000, being the rent now due to me by you for the period from September, 2007 to January, 2008 or you are hereby required to deliver up possession of the premises, within three days after service on you of this notice, to the undersigned or the undersigned will institute legal proceedings against you, to declare a forfeiture of the lease under which you occupy said premises and to recover possession thereof, with treble rents and damages.

The undersigned does (not) elect to terminate the lease if the rent is not paid within three day. (Legal description may be inserted)

Dated: 12th of January, 2008

Aditya Singh

(Lessor)

Notice to Stop Goods In Transit

Date: 12th of January, 2008

To: Common Carrier

You are in receipt of certain goods in transit shipped by us and scheduled for delivery to one of our clients.

A copy of our shipping documents is enclosed. You are hereby instructed to stop transit of said goods, not make delivery to the consignee, and return said goods to us. We agree to pay return freight charges.

No negotiable bill of lading or document of title has been delivered to our customer (consignee).

Very Truly,

Sameer Soni

Notice to Suspend Deliveries and Request for Release

Gentlemen:

Your delivery of goods which was received by us on 12th of January, 2008, does not meet the specifications as outlined in our contract.

In as much as this merchandise does not meet our requirements, we are hereby requesting that you suspend any future deliveries as called for in our herein referenced contract and release us from that certain contract.

Due to our contractual commitments, we must supply our customer with the appropriate goods within a specified period of time which requires that we now proceed to make our purchases from a different source.

We would appreciate receiving your release as soon as possible.

Yours,

Raj Singh

Notification of Returned Merchandise Credit

Dear Harsh,

Having received the merchandise you returned, we are pleased to advise you that we have credited your account in the amount of Rs. 5,00,000. If you would prefer that we mail you our cheque for the full amount of the refund, please advise us and we will be most happy to do so.

Lalit Upadhyay

■

9

Promotional Letters

Promotional Letter, Equipment Leasing

Dear Som,

Your business experience has already shown you some of the advantages of leasing needed equipment as opposed to purchasing. Our leasing experience gives us a real edge in furnishing your firm some maximum advantages with a minimum of "red tape" and time delay.

We realize the importance in properly structuring a Personalized Lease so that it may meet the specific needs and requirements of your company in the most beneficial way possible. Due to our size, we can also offer our customers the option of rewriting existing leases at certain points along the way, should it be warranted.

Please contact us if you are even considering the future acquisition of more income producing equipment and we will be most happy to speak with you either personally or by telephone, whichever you prefer.

Yours Truly,

Harshit Kumar

Promotional Letter, Air Conditioning Service

Dear Sukhpal,

Before the hot summer is upon us, we are recommending that our customers call us to arrange to have one of our service representatives perform a thorough and complete inspection of their air-conditioning systems.

Throughout our many years of experience we have learned that by taking certain preventive measures such as correcting a minor electrical problem, costly repairs and replacement of parts can often be avoided. Another reason we have for suggesting this inspection at this time is the fact that invariably it is during the hottest period of the summer that we are inundated with service requests. When this occurs, we are unable to provide quick service to all of our valued customers such as you.

Won't you give us a call so we can ensure you of a cool and comfortable summer?

Yours Truly,

Ravender

Promotional Letter, Air Freight

Dear Somesh,

Thank you for choosing our firm to deliver your air freight.

We thought you might be interested in knowing that we can make deliveries anywhere in the world and most of our overseas deliveries can be made overnight, directly to the address of the recipient. While the cost for this service will vary depending on the ultimate destination of your package, our prices are highly competitive. You may be surprised to find out just how economical this service can be.

Again, we thank you for being able to provide our service to you, and will be looking forward to serving you in the near future.

Yours Truly,

Subodh Kant

Promotional Letter, Bank

Dear Shailesh,

Let me take this opportunity to personally thank you for choosing our bank to handle your account. I know a great amount of care goes into choosing a banker, and your decision reaffirms my belief in the old fashioned ways of banking. We believe our depositors enjoy the personal contact they receive at each one of our branches.

Be assured that the personal banking concept enjoys our greatest commitment. We employ the latest technology in computers, however, we will never abandon our personal commitment to you, the customer, our greatest asset.

I hope you will investigate our trust services, and feel free to use any of the many services we have designed to make your banking experience as enjoyable and comprehensive as possible.

I have enclosed our latest financial statement for your review, along with a descriptive brochure of the many services available to you.

If I may be of any help in the future, please feel free to call upon this office.

Yours Truly,

Manoj Karnatak

Promotional Letter, Book Seller

Dear Nalin,

Someone once said that words are cheap, but he obviously did not know what he was talking about. A poorly written letter to a business associate, potential customer or dissastisfied user can be extremely costly.

Our publication, "How To Improve Your Image Through Writing", offers the reader the opportunity to compare the good letter with the bad, to put himself in the place of the recipient and judge for himself, the kind of reaction he would have on receiving that type of correspondence.

We are so confident that you will enjoy our publication, that we are offering to you the opportunity to inspect and read, if you like, this book for 10 days prior to making your commitment to either purchase or return it to us.

By returning the enclosed card, we will mail your copy of "How To Improve Your Image Through Writing" to you immediately. Do not send any money. If you decide to keep this book after 10 days, we will bill you for the purchase.

Please fill out your card today.

Yours Truly,

Akhilesh Kumar

Promotional Letter, Domestic Services

Dear Sudhir,

Wouldn't it be nice to take the day off and return to find your floors and furniture polished, carpets vacuumed, bathrooms scrubbed, beds made, oven and refrigerator cleaned and kitchen spotless?

XYZ corporations can do all of this for you for the low price. Our professionals are bonded and courteous and we know that you will be more than satisfied with the results.

We also have professionals available seven days a week to attend to your bartending and catering needs. We will be happy to provide you with these rates upon request.

Our services are available upon 24 hour notice and we will be looking forward to the opportunity to serve you.

Anand Srivastava

(XYZ Corporations)

Promotional Letter, Corporate Security

Gentlemen:

There is no doubt that without thieves, the world would be a nicer place to live. Just imagine not having to lock your doors at home, put your car in the garage, find a place for your valuables, or even stop the delivery of the newspaper when you are out of town. These habits have become an integrated part of our lives because we recognize that we are all potential victims and we do not live in a utopia.

The thief who takes off with a television, stereo, jewelry and silver has one basic motive—money. While there is always a fairly well accepted value to the "loot", this is not true when a thief has stolen proprietary information from your firm. How do you assess the value of the damage?

Unlike the home burglar, the corporate thief's motivation is not necessarily limited to self-enrichment. He may be operating off of feelings of bitterness, revenge, ego-fulfillment, daring or paying off an old debt.

Chambers Information Systems operates on a two-fold level. One, is the evaluation of your existing security system, operations and the methods for improvement. The second is a screening of personnel who have access to security sensitive areas. This study can be effectively accomplished without the awareness of any of your personnel.

Through the last few years we have discovered that as businesses grow there is often a greater need for additional security measures. Our job is to seal up the cracks and to keep items of a proprietary nature where they belong, in your possession!

We will be happy to provide you with references and anticipated costs. You are invited to contact us at your earliest convenience.

M. Ravish

(Chambers Information Systems)

Promotional Letter, Insurance

Dear Hema,

Insurance rates are competitive! Before you renew your existing Group Medical Insurance package, we would like to take a moment of your time to let you know what's been going on at Gold life Insurance.

We offer a complete medical plan, including: Life and Accidental Death Coverage, 80% Major Medical with Stop Loss and Accident benefit. We take pride in being able to offer this coverage for these low rates and in our reputation for handling claims in a speedy and efficient manner, with the least amount of paper work possible.

Thank you for giving me this moment. For more information on Gold life Insurance Plan, please call any of our service representatives at (011) 24574488.

Yours Truly,

Archana Bansal

(Gold Life Insurance)

Promotional Letter, Service Business

Dear Ravishankar,

Our firm recently received an extremely favourable review from one of the top publications, which we hope may be of some interest to you. In case you missed reading it, I have enclosed a copy with this letter.

Since our service lends itself so well to your type of business, we would appreciate having an opportunity to speak with you or one of your representatives about how we can help you to cut down on unnecessary overhead expenditures.

Please contact me at (011) 25478956, so that we can arrange a convenient time to meet. I will be looking forward to your call.

Yours Truly,

Jatin Gandhi

Promotional Letter, Public Relations

Dear Sohan,

So many questions still remain about so many historic people and happenings because word of mouth has the tremendous power of creating legends of its own.

We have mounted campaigns for relatively obscure firms that have resulted in their becoming known and sought out as major entities in their respective fields of industry. Through the placement of articles in local and national publications, in conjunction with an advertising campaign, these firms have achieved the recognition and place within the industry that would have taken many years to achieve without a public relations promotion.

We would appreciate having the opportunity to speak with you personally and discuss some of our ideas for promoting our company, City Promotions, please call me at my number (011) 25478956 in order to set up a convenient time for me to come and see you.

Yours Truly,

Sudhir Gupta

■

10

Reply and Referral Letters

Reply Notice of Reshipment

Dear Mohan,

Thank you for your letter informing us that the item you ordered had not arrived.

We are sorry for the inconvenience this has caused and have arranged to have another one sent to you today. In the event that the original order is delivered to you, please call the toll-free number listed on our letterhead. We have notified our shipping agent in an attempt to discover why this problem occurred. Please accept our apology and thanks for placing your order with us.

Yours Truly,

Prashant Bhushan

Reply Apology and Notice of Shipment in Replacement

Dear Raj

Your letter has been received, and we were very sorry to hear about the problem you experienced with our product. We maintain rigid inspection standards, but occasionally an imperfection does slip by, as it unfortunately did in the case of your product. We have entered a replacement order to be shipped to you at once. Your satisfaction is extremely important to us and we apologize for the inconvenience you have been caused.

Thank you for purchasing our products.

Yours Truly,

Manish Mehta

Reply and New Customer Welcome

Dear Aftab,

Your letter just arrived, and after reading it several times to be absolutely sure of its content, I can say how pleased I am with your decision to purchase your plywood products from us.

Ours is truly a business whose future depends upon the satisfaction of our customers. Welcome to that family.

You can rest assured that we will strive to provide you with the fastest most efficient service, along with the highest quality products available.

Should you have any problems, or any ideas on ways that we can improve our service, please feel free to call upon me. Again, welcome aboard.

Yours Truly,

Pawan Kumar

Reply and Referral to Distributor

Dear John,

Thank you for your recent inquiry regarding where our products can be purchased in your country.

We have not yet established foreign distribution for our products, and therefore they can only be presently purchased from our distributor. If you are interested in placing an order for any of our merchandise, you can direct your correspondence to us.

We have forwarded a copy of your letter to our distributor in order to acquaint him with your needs and requirements should you decide to place an order.

Thank you very much for the interest you have exhibited in our products. If we can be of any more assistance to you, please call upon our office at any time.

Yours,

Akshay Anand

Reply to Notice of Item Missing from Carton

Dear Satish,

Your letter informing us that the missing item for your new product was not included in the carton has been brought to my attention.

There is a package on its way to you now that includes the item and a little something extra. This is our way of saying how sorry we are for having slipped up, and thanking you for choosing the product.

If I can be of assistance to you in any way in the future, please call us at any time.

Yours Truly,

Vinay Ahuja,

Reply to Inquiry and Inability to Offer Substitute

Dear Lalit,

Your letter inquiring about one of our product was brought to my attention.

While we manufacture a vast assortment of products, none of our models fit the description which you provided. You may wish to direct an inquiry to our distributor in your city, whose firm has been in existence for many years and who may have the answer you are seeking:

I am sorry that I am unable to be of more assistance to you. Best of luck!

Yours Truly,

Deepak Joshi

Reply to Request about Credit Rejection

Date: 21st of September, 2007

To: Shyam Saran

In response to your request for a statement of our reasons for turning down your recent application for credit, our records reveal that your application was not approved for certain undisclosed reasons.

We appreciate your patronage and invite you to shop with us on a cash basis.

Very Truly,

Vinay Pathak

Reply Cancelling Unfilled Order

Dear Sudhanshu,

I am in receipt of your correspondence noticing us that there will be a two week delay in the shipment of the merchandise.

This delay is unacceptable and we are therefore cancelling our purchase order for the ordered items.

Yours,

Deepak Sehgal

Reply to Inquiry about Discontinued Model

Dear Shyam,

The reason that you have been unable to find our product and model no., is because this model has been discontinued. We replaced it with new model number, which offers the same fine quality that our customers have come to expect.

I am enclosing a list of the stores in your area where our products can be purchased, and would like to thank you for choosing our product.

Yours Truly,

Anand John

Reply Notice of Shipment Being Traced

Dear Anand,

Your lighter was repaired on April 19th and was shipped on April 20th. We can only assume that the lighter was lost in transit.

Upon receipt of your letter, we reported the loss immediately to the carrier and they are attempting to locate the parcel. We should have a report back within two weeks. If ABC is successful in locating your lighter, then it will be forwarded to you promptly. If, after two weeks, they have been unsuccessful, we will forward a cheque to you for the value of the lighter.

We are sorry for the inconvenience this has caused you.

Yours Truly,

Mohan Kumar

Referral of Account to Collection Agency

Gentlemen:

This debtor has not responded to our requests for payment. Our only alternative now is the actual placing of the account for collection.

As a final courtesy to this firm, we ask that you take no drastic steps toward collection until 30th of June. If we do receive payment in full by this date, we will notify you to cancel the claim. Otherwise, you are to proceed in any manner you deem advisable to collect our money. A statement of account is attached and a copy of this letter is being sent to the debtor so that they will have ample time to pay before the expiration of the date.

Yours,

Monish Mathur

■

11

Request Letters

Request for Additional Information Not in Brochure

Dear Lalit,

On 5th of February, 2006, I requested information on your new software package, and your brochure was delivered to my office on 25th of the same month.

Thank you for the manner in which you expedited this information to me. You are to be commended. I do have one question regarding your new program. I am sending a letter regarding this question. I will be looking forward to your response.

Yours,

Abhinav Kumar

Request for Advertising Rate Information

Dear Sumit,

We are interested in investigating the possibility of national advertising for one of our products. We would be very appreciative if you would provide us with your rates and any demographic information you may have on potential users for our products.

Thank you for your prompt attention to our request. We will be looking forward to hearing from you.

Yours,

Shantanu Anand

Request for Authorisation to Substitute

Dear Bikash,

This is to inform you that the agreement between you and our firm to supply certain goods is facing some sort of problems because the unavailability of certain goods.

We regret to inform you that the goods are unavailable because of some unavoidable reasons.

We are hereby requesting your authorisation to substitute these products in lieu of some of other equally good products.

If you are agreeable to this, would you please acknowledge your acceptance by letter.

We will look forward to your response.

Yours Truly,

Kaushik Awasthi

Request for Credit Application

Dear Amit,

Our firm, ABC Sales, is interested in opening an account with your establishment. We carry an extensive line of computer hardware and software and service the greater part of Central India.

Would you please provide us with a current catalogue, price list, information regarding your billing procedures and a credit application.

I will be looking forward to receiving this material in the near future.

Yours,

Santosh Narang

Request for Credit Information

Dear Amit,

It was with great pleasure that we received your recent order which was entered for immediate shipment at our regular 30 day terms.

To enable us to extend the line of credit you may need for future orders, will you send us the usual credit information? We have enclosed a simplified financial statement form for your convenience.

Thank you again for your order. We are looking forward to a long and mutually rewarding business relationship.

Yours Truly,

Lalit Kapoor

Request for Credit and Pickup of Merchandise Delivered Late

Dear Akash,

The merchandise that we ordered from you on March 27th, was delivered on May 17th, which was two days after our sale had ended. What is most regrettable is the fact that I believe if we had the merchandise on hand for the sale, we could have sold three or four cases.

I understand that you were experiencing some internal problems during this period. I am, however, unwilling to keep the six cases that were just delivered due to the delay. Two cases will suffice for now and I would appreciate it if you would have someone call for the remainder and credit my account accordingly.

Thank you for your prompt attention to this matter.

Yours,

Hem Kandpal

Request for Clarification on Applying Payment

Dear Hem,

In order to assist our accounts receivable department personnel, we request that you please include your statement stub with your payment and place a check mark next to those invoices you are including in your payment.

This will enable proper crediting of your account.

Thank you very much.

Yours Truly,

Pawan Singh

Request for Disclosure of Credit History and Inquiries

Dear Aman,

Request is hereby made for your disclosure to me of the nature and substance of all information, other than medical, presently in your files, pertaining to my credit history.

I also request disclosure of all sources of said information, and the names of the firms which have requested a consumer report on me and have been furnished same by you within the limits prescribed by law.

These requests are in accordance with my rights under federal law. Your cooperation in this matter is appreciated.

Yours Truly,

Kris Sharma

Request for Estimate of Appraisal Costs

Dear Manoj,

One of the requirements for obtaining refinancing on my property , is to obtain a current appraisal for the lender, who is Mr. Seth.

The location of the property which is to be appraised is 13th Street, Malviya Nagar, Delhi and the appraisal is to be based on the land value plus improvements.

I would appreciate your providing me with an estimate of both time and costs in order for you to prepare an appraisal that will meet the lender's requirements.

If you have any questions regarding this appraisal, please give us a call. Thank you.

Yours Truly,

Santosh Kumar

Request for Extension of Time on Promissory Note

Dear Mukul,

According to the terms and conditions of the promissory note I signed on June 15, 2007, I am obligated to tender my payment in the amount of Rs.50,000 to you on June 15, 2007.

I have just been informed that funds which were to be paid to me prior to the due date on the note, have been delayed. Needless to say, this comes as a great disappointment to me. I have been assured, however, that these funds will be in my possession by June 7, 2007.

I am requesting that the due date on the promissory note be extended for a period of one month and a just consideration for said extension be suggested by you.

I will look forward to your early response.

Yours,

Saurabh Singh

Request for Full Refund

Dear Pawan,

The product I purchased from you on September 2, 2008 turned out to be quite a disappointment. While it looked the same as the one I saw in your commercial, it did not perform in the same way.

Following the instructions, I placed an onion in its proper position and pushed down on the mincer, which immediately bent out of shape. I experienced the same problem when I attempted to dice a carrot.

Therefore, I am returning this product to you and ask that you issue me a full refund. I am not interested in receiving a replacement.

Yours Truly,

Deepak Kumar

Request for Information in Advance of Purchase Order

Dear Shyam,

Attached to this letter is an overview of those items and services which we anticipate ordering from your firm, providing your terms and conditions are favourable, and your prices competitive. Since this is only an informed guess as to our needs, it should not be considered as anything more than a rough idea of our requirements.

Please provide to us, in writing, a price list, along with your terms and conditions of sale, applicable discounts, shipping dates and additional sales and corporate policies. Should the information you provide be acceptable and competitive, you can look forward to our first order within thirty (30) days.

Thank you for you cooperation. We have also enclosed our procurement specifications and conditions for your review.

Yours Truly,

Abhigyan Adarsh

Request for Instructions on Deferred Collections

Dear Suket,

May we please have your latest instructions on this account? We ask this because collection has been deferred at your request.

Please let us know if any payments have been made so that we can update our files accordingly. If there have been no payments tendered, we need to know how you wish us to proceed in your behalf.

For your convenience, you may write your comments here:

Thank you for your cooperation.

Yours,

Kapil Kumar

Request for Proof of Merchandise Return

Dear Anoushan,

In reference to your letter , we have no record of having received the merchandise you returned.

In order to issue you a refund for the Rs. 80,000, we request that you provide us with the following information:

1. Date you returned the merchandise
2. Form of shipment
3. Copies of any correspondence to us in regard to returning merchandise

Your cooperation in this matter will enable us to trace the parcel.

Thank you for your help. I will be looking forward to your letter.

Yours,

Shyam Sunder

Request for Refund on Undelivered Merchandise

Dear Saket,

In my letter of 21st of September, 2007, I explained that the merchandise I ordered from you hadn't arrived. I am attaching a copy of that correspondence for your convenience.

Having received neither the merchandise nor a response to my previous letter, I am requesting that you refund the amount remitted with my order. Attached is a copy of my cancelled cheque.

I shall be looking forward to receiving my refund promptly. Thank you for your immediate attention to this matter.

Yours,

Sunder Aiyer

Request for Replacement of Cheque on Pending Order

Dear Alam,

This to acknowledge the receipt of your cheque for your pending order. Thank you very much.

Unfortunately, this cheque is not drawn in accordance with our contractual terms for payment and we are, therefore, returning it to you.

Would you please authorize the issuance of a replacement cheque in accordance with the provisions for payment?

We are most anxious to deliver and will be looking forward to hearing from you in the near future.

Yours,

M. Husain

Request to Locate Former Employee

Dear Sudhir,

For some time I have been unsuccessfully attempting to locate an individual who was previously in your employ. His name is Ramesh Thakur and I have been informed that he worked for you during September 2006 to December 2006.

If you know his current whereabouts, I would appreciate your either informing me of same or forwarding this letter to him.

Thank you very much for your help in this matter.

Yours Truly,

Aman Malhotra

Request for Wholesale Price List

Dear Santosh,

Your advertisement in March issue of a popular magazine is of great interest to us.

We would like to know more about the products your firm offers and would appreciate receiving your wholesale price list and information regarding terms and ordering policy.

It is our desire to offer our customers the widest selection possible of the product, and we are therefore always interested in new products that fall within that area.

We will look forward to your prompt response. Thank you.

Yours Truly,

Deepak Mehrotra

Request to Include Landlord in Tenant's Liability Insurance

Dear Adarsh,

In case you have not had an opportunity to read through the Lease, please note that there is an insurance clause that requires the tenant to carry public liability insurance of Rs. 50,000 and property damage insurance of Rs. 100,000. The landlord must be named as additional insured.

In as much as we are sub-leasing these offices to you, please have named also, and ask your agent to send us a notice to that effect.

Thank you very much.

Yours,

Sidharth Vinayak

Request for Warranty Repair

Dear Anmol,

The watch that is within this parcel was purchased on November 2, 2006, and is under warranty. The problem that I am encountering is that the watch fails to keep accurate time. It seems to gain approximately five minutes per hour.

Please make any adjustments necessary, and return to the above address as soon as possible.

Yours Truly,

Karan Singh

■

12

Response and Return Letters

Response to Improper Billing After Payment

Dear Kunal,

On 21st of May, I received your letter which indicated that I had a balance owing Rs. 50,000.

On 25th of the same month, I mailed a cheque for Rs. 80,000.

You should have received my cheque prior to writing your letter and I am, therefore, somewhat concerned.

If you have not received my cheque by the time this letter arrives, I would appreciate hearing from you in as much as I should issue a stop payment on the funds.

I will hold this matter in abeyance until I hear from you.

Yours,

Abhishek Sah

Response to Invoice Received After Payment

Dear Shantanu,

This is to acknowledge our receipt of your invoice.

A cheque of our records indicates that payment for this invoice was made with our cheque no. 546892 payable to you in the amount of Rs. 50,000.

Please review your records and bank deposits to be sure that you have not received our payment. If you are still unable to find a record of payment, let me know, and I will request a photocopy of our cheque, and forward it to your office. This normally takes about 30 days. If I do not hear from you, I will assume that you have found our payment and have appropriately credited our account.

Yours,

Kunal Singh

Third Letter in Response to Billing Error

Dear Naresh,

This is the third letter that I have written to you regarding the status of my account.

I am enclosing copies of my previous letters to avoid having to set forth the same information for you again. I am beginning to get quite annoyed by all of the dunning notices you have been sending to me in error and would greatly appreciate if someone would straighten out the problem that exists on your end. I do understand the difficulty you must have in maintaining all of your records, but I do believe that if you would bring my correspondence to the attention of your credit manager he may decide to suspend the mailing of these notices to me until this problem is resolved.

Thank you.

Yours,

Lalit Kumar

Response to Order on Expired Credit Card

Dear Deepak,

Thank you for your recent order.

We are unable to send you the merchandise due to the fact that your credit card has expired.

If you still want, please forward your cheque or other acceptable form of payment and we will be happy to send the order immediately.

Thank you.

Mukul Pant

Response to Notice in Regard to Cancelled Coverage

Dear Hardayal,

This correspondence is to inform you that your subject notice, is of little effect, in fact, it canceled on 22nd of May, 2006. We wish to advise you that this oversight on your part shall in no way accrue an earned premium or short rate due by this insured.

If you are in disagreement with the information, please direct any future correspondence to my attorney.

Yours,

Lalit Sen

Response to Request for Interest Paid Information

Dear Shyam,

In response to your recent request concerning interest made on your loan during 2005, our records indicate that the amount of interest paid to our note department was Rs. 80,000.

We are enclosing a copy of our original statement sent to you for your records.

Yours,

Kamal Garg

Response to Request for Service on Expired Warranty

Dear Khushi,

We are sorry to hear about the problem you have had with your product. We would like to be able to make the necessary adjustments at no charge to you, but, unfortunately, the warranty is expired.

The proof of purchase you mailed to us indicates that the product was purchased on 21st of December, 2007. Since our warrnaty is good for a period of one year from the date of purchase, it expired three months ago.

If you would like us to repair the product for you, there will be a charge for this. We will guarantee the work we do for a period of 6 months.

Please check the appropriate box on the enclosed instruction card and return it to us as soon as possible.

Yours,

Sammer Singh

Response to Inquiry Concerning Former Employee, with Reference

Dear Akash,

This is to acknowledge receipt of your inquiry in which you requested information regarding a previous employee of our firm.

Ms. Mondal was my personal secretary for the last three years. She is intelligent, dependable and extremely well organized. She is fastidious in her appearance and is very conscientious about her work.

Yours Truly,

Deepak Kumar

Return Authorisation

Dear Lokesh,

Your letter of 20th December, 2007 in which you described the condition of the item you ordered from us has been brought to my attention. We are very sorry that this merchandise was damaged in transit.

Please return the damaged goods to us by placing the original carton inside a slightly larger box and attaching a copy of your letter to us on the outside of the package. Upon receipt of the merchandise, we will immediately send you a replacement and a cheque to reimburse you for the extra shipping expense.

I am sorry for this inconvenience, but this procedure must be followed for insurance purposes.

Thank you for your understanding and patience.

Yours Truly,

Hem Upadhyay

Return of Purchase Order and Request for Advance Payment

Dear Amit,

Your purchase order has been referred to me. I note that the third item on the order is 50,000 of our Model 310 Flags at a price of Rs. 10 each. While we appreciate an order of this size, the terms and conditions of our catalogue clearly specify that orders are accepted with full payment in advance, and with an amount sufficient to cover sending charges.

We are therefore returning your purchase order. Please resubmit your order with either a sight draft, or an irrevocable letter of credit. We anticipate sending charges to be in the neighbourhood of Re.1.00 per flag ordered.

Thank you for your order. We look forward to serving you in the near future.

Yours,

Mayank Tripathi

Return of Cheque Missing Signature

Dear Saket,

We thank you for your cheque in the amount of Rs. 53650. Our enthusiasm was somewhat dampened when we noticed the absence of the authorized signature on the bottom of the cheque.

Naturally, we presume this is a mere oversight and are enclosing the cheque in question for your signature. A postage paid envelope is provided herein for your convenience.

Thank you for your prompt attention to this matter.

Yours Truly,

Aman Sinha

Return of Late Payment and Denial of Discount

Dear Somesh,

Your cheque of Rs. 60,000 is being returned to you because it has been made out for the wrong amount.

As we have explained previously, the 2% discount we offer can only be applied when your payment is mailed within 10 days of delivery. By waiting beyond that period, you forego the opportunity to deduct the discount from the amount of your invoice.

Since your payment of the invoice was not made within the specified time period, you are not entitled to a discount on this order.

We are appreciative of your business and are most willing to accommodate you in any way possible. Our policy, however, in regard to open account terms, is strict, and in fairness to all of our customers, must be even handed.

Please remit your cheque for the full amount of the invoice. Your cooperation in this matter is appreciated.

Thank you for your understanding.

Yours,

Ashish Kumar

■

13

Letters of Thanks

Thank You for Customer Referral

Dear Somit,

Mr. Gupte has retained me to represent him.

During our initial conference, he informed me that he had chosen our firm based upon your recommendation. I want to thank you for this referral and inform you that I believe we will be able to assist in this matter.

I am pleased that everything has worked out so well for you.

Yours Truly,

Dinesh Singh

Thank You for Favourable Product Review

Dear Amit,

Thank you for the favourable review you gave our new product.

We are pleased that you found our product very useful. We certainly enjoyed reading your review and would like to thank you once again for your kind words.

Yours Truly,

Shisir Narang

Thank You for Evaluation Product, Product Unacceptable

Dear Hem,

Thank you for submitting the product to the firm for evaluation.

Based on the results of our technical evaluation, our review committee has made the decision not to accept your product for distribution at this time. Should you have any questions about the evaluation process, please submit them, in writing, attention Product Services Department. Unfortunately, because of our current workload, we are unable to respond to requests for information on the telephone.

Should you develop or wish to submit other products in the future that you feel may be of interest to us, please feel free to contact us. Again, thank you for considering the firm as a potential distributor.

Yours Truly,

Krishna Kant

Thank You for Offer to Help Us Campaign

Dear Sharath,

Your offer to help us in our campaign to eliminate poverty is greatly appreciated. If everyone were to commit themselves with the same level of enthusiasm you expressed in your letter, we would undoubtedly have this problem licked in no time at all.

We are sending you one hundred of our pamphlets to be distributed to your personnel. This will help us to spread the word while keeping our costs down to a minimum. Thank you again for your willingness to assist.

Yours Truly,

Himanshu Pandey

Thank You for Hiring

Dear Adarsh,

Thank you for giving me the opportunity to prove my capabilities with your firm.

I want to thank you for the expression of faith in my abilities that you have exhibited by this gesture and will certainly do my very best not to disappoint you.

Yours Truly,

Krishna Gupta

Thank You for Interview

Dear Hyder,

Thank you for the time and consideration you extended to me during my interview with you yesterday. I appreciate having had the opportunity to speak with you about my experience in related fields and my future goals.

I shall look forward to hearing from you and wish to thank you again for your courtesy.

Yours Truly,

Shyam Gupta

Thank You for Offer to Help, Accepted

Dear Mukul,

Your offer of help is truly appreciated at this time. I believe if we can get our cost estimates down, we should be able to have this proposal ready to submit by the June 1st deadline. I know that by taking you up on your kind offer, we will both be burning the midnight oil for the next week and a half, but I really doubt that I will be able to complete this within the time limit without your help.

Thank you very much.

Yours,

Subodh Singh

Thank You for Payment After Phone Call

Dear Jagdish,

Your letter of 3rd March in which you enclosed your payment of Rs. 15,000 has been received and I would like to thank you for your prompt remittance following our telephone call of the same date.

Thank you for the kind words contained in your letter. We look forward to many years of mutual prosperity.

Yours,

Karan Rastogi

Thank You for Support During Illness

Dear Adarsh,

Heart attacks are something that happen to the next fellow, and it was therefore rather surprising to wake up in General Hospital and be informed that I had just had one.

I have learned of the generous support you lent to my family during my illness, and would like to sincerely thank you for the kindness and assistance you provided during my immobility. Individuals like you are few and far between. I am looking forward to returning to work as soon as I get my clean bill of health. Thank you again.

Yours,

Akash Sehgal

Thank You for Tour

Dear Deepak,

Having been guided on a tour of your plant by Mr. Gupta, I must say that I am thoroughly impressed with your operations and personnel. I don't believe I have ever viewed a more efficient, smooth running, and cost efficient programme such as yours. I was particularly impressed with the procedure you have implemented to monitor quality control.

All of your employees were extremely courteous and went out of their way to explain various functions and answer my inquiries. I would be most appreciative if you would extend a special thank you from me to Mr. Gupta, for showing me every courtesy.

I shall be presenting my findings to my associates on the 30th, and will let you know what develops.

Yours,

Aditya Singh

Thank You for The Opportunity, Service Business

Dear Lalit,

Thank you for providing with the opportunity to be of service to you.

It is my sincere hope that you are completely satisfied with the service which was provided to you and will avail yourself of our expertise again in the future.

We are always interested in suggestions that would allow us to improve upon our already high standards and encourage you to submit your thoughts. Again, thank you.

Your

Deepak Singh

Thank You for Your Confidence, Service Business

Dear Kartik,

Thank you for your confidence in our ability to serve you. We welcome the opportunity to assist you in your business and look forward to a continuing relationship which will be profitable to all concerned. Our staff is available to you. Should the need arise, please give us a call.

Yours,

Dinesh Kumar

Thank You for Your Inquiry, Price List Enclosed

Dear Shyamal,

Your letter of inquiry regarding our product line has been brought to my attention and I would like to thank you for your interest in some of company's products.

I have enclosed a price list and data sheets which describe our full line of products that serve the industry. This should help to familiarize you with our family of products and the high quality of our equipment. If you have any further questions about any of the firm's products, please call us at our toll-free number, 911- 25478945

Thank you again for your interest.

Yours Truly,

Abhimanyu Singh

Thank You for Your Kind Comments

Dear Pratik,

Thank you for your kind comments on the performance of our product. As you may know, so few people take the time to let a manufacturer know when they are satisfied with a product. Your letter has been sent to Japan where one of my colleagues will post it with a Japanese translation on the employee bulletin board.

Don't be surprised if you get a few thank you letters from the employees, as they pride themselves in the quality of their work and love to hear from our family of customers.

Yours Truly,

Manoj Joshi

Christmas Season Thank You to Valued Customers

Dear Customer,

As the Christmas season approaches, there is always so much activity and personal business to attend to that it is easy to forget to thank our valued customers, like you, for their orders.

So before I forget, thank you, and may this holiday season bring to you and your family all of the joy and happiness that you deserve.

Yours,

Henry Martin

Thanksgiving Letter to Customers

Dear Customer,

We are always happy when Thanksgiving is approaching, because this wonderful holiday affords us the opportunity to thank all of our friends. This past year has been good to us, and we thank you for your patronage and for allowing us to be of service to you.

Happy Thanksgiving.

Yours Truly,

Frank Malthus

■

14

E-mails

Seeking Information about Computer

Dear Sir/Madam,

I'd like some more information about the computer you're selling. I'm in the market for a particular type of computer which suits my needs and I saw your advertisement. Please reply to this message with information about the computer's RAM, its hard drive size, its processor speed, whether or not it has a modem or a CD/DVD drive, and if you are including any software.

Most importantly, let me know if your price is negotiable. Please send a reply e-mail as soon as possible. If everything looks good I'll contact you and perhaps we can do business.

Of course, if the computer has already been sold, please let me know. Thanks very much.

Adarsh Srivastava

New Delhi

Information about Financial Product

Dear Sir/Madam,

I learned about some of your financial products recently from a reputed daily and was intrigued. I would like to get further information about your offer and what it entails. Please send more information to the address below. I would like to know about interest rates, tax deductions, points, and other vital information.

If you can, simply send me an e-mail with that information. Thank you for your attention to this matter. I hope to hear from you soon, and I hope we can do business.

Pranav Kant

12, Mayur Vihar
New Delhi

Seeking Information about Internet Service Provider

Dear Sir/Madam,

It seems like Internet service providers are competing not for the growing number of Netizens, but to see who can provide the worst customer service. I'm fed up with my current provider, so I'd like to get information about what you can do for me. I'm looking for a new provider. That's not too much. If you offer any additional services, that would be icing on the cake.

Please reply with information about your pricing, your setup software, and your local servers. The faster you get back to me, the more likely I am to go with you as my new ISP. I'll also tell my unhappy friends about you.

Khushi Mehrotra

New Delhi

Seeking Information about Legislation

Dear Sir/Madam,

I recently read about the piece of legislation and saw that this proposed law will soon come up for a vote before legislative body. Since this proposal could have a profound effect on me, I wish to find out more about it and learn whether or not I wish to support it. In that spirit, I am requesting any appropriate information about the legislation that you can send me.

This may be in the form of newspaper articles, legal drafts or other documents. Any information will help me decide whether or not I can support this legislation, and whether I should contact my representative about it. Please send any information to the address below as soon as possible. If necessary, contact me and I will pay for the postage. Thank you for your attention to this matter.

Raman Pal

New Delhi

Information about Product

Dear Sir/Madam,

Please send me all the information available about your new product. I recently saw some information about this product and it interested me enough to warrant my contacting you. This product may fill a need that I currently have and if it proves to be reasonably priced, well-made and backed by a reputable company, I will almost certainly become a customer of yours.

Please send any brochures or other information to the address below. I look forward to receiving your material. Thank you for your time.

Pranav Kant

New Delhi

Information about Real Estate

Dear Sir/Madam,

I'm thinking of purchasing a new home in the next three months and would like to receive information about your properties. I've seen ads and other publicity about your new community, and the homes look like something that might suit both my tastes and my family's needs. If you could, please send information about the following: models, prices, financing, custom options, shopping, cultural opportunities, schools, and traffic.

You can send the information to the address below, or direct me to a web site if that's appropriate. Thank you for your attention. I look forward to learning more about your properties.

Pranav Kant

Information about Website

Dear Sir/Madam,

I wanted to tell you how much I liked your Web site. I was very impressed with the design, the writing, and the overall feel of it. You should be very proud of creating such an outstanding site. I would love to get more information about how you created your site: how you created the graphics, how you did the programming, and that sort of thing. I think I could learn a lot from you.

If it's not too much trouble, could you please reply to my message with some of that information? And if you like, refer me to some of the people who created the site for you? That would also be a big help. In return, I'll tell everyone I know who's online about your site. I hope to hear from you soon. Great work!

Yours Truly,

Pranav Kant

Seeking Information about Company

Dear Sir/Madam,

I'm e-mailing you to get some more information about your company. I plan to be engaged with your firm in the near future, and I would appreciate finding out more about your firm. If you could, please reply with some information about the company's background, its people, its primary market, and any other pertinent information. Or if there is an online source of this information, please direct me to that.

I thank you for your help, and appreciate your cooperation. I will look forward to your reply.

Yours Truly,

Lalit Kumar

Command to Stop Online Flaming Discussions

Hello,

Did you not get the idea from my last message asking you to stop sending your puerile, obnoxious messages to our group? Apparently, we can't appeal to your sense of decency and fair play, and we would never resort to threats, so let me just tell you this: We laugh at you. Your messages are the subject of ridicule and derision. Your opinions are ripped apart and you're called unpleasant names by even the gentlest of us. Do you get the idea?

If you think you're having an effect on our opinions or our minds, you're not. All you're doing is making a fool of yourself. If you want to continue sending us your asinine messages, there's nothing else we can do to stop you, other than to say that you're wasting your time. We don't listen, we never will, and I'll waste no more time e-mailing you.

Prempal Yadav

Response to Flame about Recent Message

Hello,

I always thought the Internet was supposed to be a place for expression of ideas, no matter what they are! Boy, I guess I was wrong! Your flame e-mail message was an overreaction. I was shocked to find such an angry message in my mailbox, and I'm still not sure what I did to warrant it.

If you or someone else in the group didn't agree with what I said about that subject I respect that. Tell me so, and let's talk. Maybe you can change my mind.

But don't go sending me such vicious e-mails as if I was advocating burning the Constitution! It's unnecessary and rude. You may want to respond and rethink your tone. Go ahead. I'm sure I can find others more open to ideas that don't agree with theirs.

Parul Jain

Thank You for Civilised Flame

Hello,

I was pleasantly surprised to receive from you what would be called by many Netizens a "flame". I was surprised that even though you didn't agree with my ideas or my opinions about this subject you told me so in a mannered, intelligent, classy way. In an era of incredibly rude, vulgar e-mails sent by equally rude, vulgar people, your "flame" was refreshing.

I would love to debate with you more directly about this topic. It seems to me that you're an educated, quick-witted person who knows how to partake in civilized discourse, and I think we'd have a lot of fun going back and forth about the issues. Feel free to e-mail me with your opinions on this subject as a starting point. Thanks again for your polite message. I hope to enjoy skewering you very soon.

Pranav Kant

General Congratulation Mail

Dear Saurabh,

Congratulations! I wasn't surprised at all when you got this success. You've been so dedicated, so hard working, and so good at kissing up to the right people that this kind of recognition was bound to come sooner or later. But seriously, it couldn't happen to a more deserving person.

Enjoy your glory and be proud of what you've accomplished. Tomorrow, you're just another grunt (just kidding). Again, my congratulations and best wishes!

Yours,

Lalit Kumar

■

15

Financial Letters

Error on Credit Card Statement

1234, Main Street
Bangalore
04 April, 2008

Dear Sir/Madam,

Re: Error on Account No. 123456

My last statement, dated 21of March 2008, contained a transaction in the amount of 50,000Rs. Please be advised that I did not charge this amount to my account and therefore wish to dispute it. Would you please check your records to verify the validity of this charge?

If you should determine that this is, indeed, a valid charge on my account, I would appreciate it if you would provide me with a copy of the original charge slip bearing my signature.

Until I receive word from you as to the results of your investigation, I will be deducting the disputed amount from my current payment.

Thank you for your attention to this matter. If you should have any questions, please do not hesitate to contact me.

Regards,

Lalit Kumar

Business Letter for Credit

1234, Main Street
Bangalore
04 April, 2008

Dear Sir/Madam,

I am the manager of Abc Company. We specialize in manufacturing of small toys. I am writing to ask that you consider this request for a line of credit with your company. To assist you in your evaluation, I am providing the following information:

BUSINESS LICENSE No.: 1245638 DOING BUSINESS SINCE: 1977

I am also enclosing letters of reference from other creditors with whom my company has a maintained an excellent and mutually beneficial relationship. Thank you for your consideration of this request. If you have any questions or need additional information, please do not hesitate to contact me.

Regards,

Jagdish Kumar

Letter to Creditor Disrupting Negative Credit Report

1234, Main Street
Bangalore
02 August, 2008

Dear Sir/Madam,

Re: Account No123456

I recently received a copy of my credit report from a credit reporting agency. That report indicates that my account with you is not properly managed.

According to my records, however, this account has always been maintained in a proper way. I would, therefore, appreciate it if you would notify to this credit reporting agency that this account is well managed and that all payments have been made on time.

Thank you for your immediate attention to this request.

Regards,

Lalit Kumar

Personal Request for Credit

123/A, Main Street
Bangalore
04 April, 2008

Dear Sir/Madam,

The purpose of this letter is to formally request a line of credit with your company. To assist you in your evaluation of this request, I am providing the following information:

FULL NAME: Lalit Kumar

DATE OF BIRTH: 31-12-1975

I would like a line of credit of Rs. 5,00,000. I would, however, be happy to discuss this amount with you. Thank you for your consideration of this request. If you have any questions or need additional information, please do not hesitate to contact me.

Regards,

Subhash Kumar

Request for Copy of Credit Report

1234, Main Street
Ahmedabad
04 April, 2008

Dear Sir/Madam,

I would appreciate it if you would please furnish me with a copy of my credit report. My full name is Lalit Kumar and my date of birth is 31-12-1975. I understand there is a fee charge for this service. Accordingly, enclosed please find my cheque made out in this amount.

I look forward to receiving the requested information.

Regards,

Lalit Kumar

Request for Balance Transfer to Account

1234, Main Street
Bangalore
04 April, 2008

Dear Sir/Madam,

Re: Balance Transfer

Account No. 254789

The purpose of this letter is to authorize you to transfer the balance from my account to another one. Details of my account number, another account number and the balance in both the accounts have been given in an attached separate paper. I would appreciate it if you would attend to this as soon as possible, and provide me with written confirmation once the transfer has been completed.

Thank you for your assistance in this matter. If you have any questions or need additional information, please do not hesitate to contact me.

Regards,

Anita Kapil

Request for Credit Report after Denial Credit

1234, Main Street
Ahmedabad
04 April, 2005

Dear Sir/Madam,

Recently, I was denied credit based upon information provided by your company. I would, therefore, appreciate being furnished with a copy of my credit report. My full name is Dinesh Chandra and my date of birth is 31-02-1975.

Thank you for your attention to this request. I look forward to receiving the requested information.

Regards,

Dinesh Chandra

Request for Increase of Credit Limit

1234, Main Street
Bangalore
04 April, 2008

Re: Increase of Credit Limit
Account No. 123456

Dear Sir/Madam,

I would appreciate it if you would consider increasing the limit on my current line of credit. As you will see from an examination of my account history, I have made payments in a consistent and timely fashion. Therefore, I request that you consider raising my credit limit from Rs. 5,00,000 to 1,000,000.

I believe you have all the information already in your files with which to evaluate this request, but if you should have any questions or need additional information, please do not hesitate to contact me.

Regards,

Lalit Kumar

Request to add Additional Party to Account

1234, Main Street
Bangalore
04 April, 2008

Re: Account No. 123456

Dear Sir/Madam,

I am writing to request that you add Lalit Kumar to the above-referenced account as a secondary cardholder. I authorize you to extend to him all the charging privileges attendant thereto. To assist you in processing this request, I am providing the following information:

FULL NAME: Lalit Kumar

ADDRESS: C-13, Laxmi Nagar, New Delhi

TELEPHONE NUMBER: 23456789

Please feel free to verify the above information by contacting at the address and phone listed above.

I appreciate your attention to this request and hope that you will contact me immediately should you have any questions.

Regards,

Rohit Kumar

Request to Close Account

1234, Main Street
Bangalore
04 April, 2005

Re: Request to Close Account

Account No. 458795

Dear Sir/Madam,

Please be advised that I wish to close the above-referenced account with your company. According to my records, the current balance on the account is Rs. 55,000. Would you please close the account and forward your final statement to me at your earliest convenience? I would appreciate confirmation in writing that the account has been closed and no further charges are authorized.

Thank you for your attention to this request. If you have any questions, please do not hesitate to contact me.

Regards,

Dinesh Chandra

Request to Remove Party from Account

1234, Main Street
Bangalore
04 April, 2008

Re: Account No. 123456

Dear Sir/Madam,

Please be advised that, as the primary account holder, I wish to have Ramesh removed from my account. Effective immediately, I request that all further charging privileges for Ramesh be revoked for this account. All future statements, correspondence and inquiries should be sent only to me at my address.

I would appreciate it if you would provide me with written confirmation that Ramesh is no longer a cardholder on this account. Thank you for your immediate attention to this request. I look forward to hearing from you.

Regards,

Lalit Kumar

Letter Confirming Payment Plan

1234, Main Street
Boston, MA 02123
04 April, 2008

Re: Account No. 258746

Dear Sir/Madam,

This letter will confirm the payment plan which we have agreed to in order to bring this account current. According to our agreement, I will make 10 payments in the amount of Rs. 20,000 each until the account is paid in full. These payments will be due on the 7th day of the month.

Thank you for your assistance and understanding in this matter. If you have any questions or if the above does not agree with you understanding of our arrangement, please notify me immediately.

Regards,

Dinesh Chandra

Letter Enclosing Partial Payment to Collection Agency

1234, Main Street
Bangalore
04 April, 2008

Re: Collections Account No. 123456

Dear Sir/Madam,

Enclosed please find my cheque number 254678 in the amount of Rs. 55,000 representing partial payment on the above-referenced account. According to our agreement, I will be making 8 additional payments until this account is paid in full.

Thank you for your assistance in this matter.

Regards,

Ayub Khan

Letter Enclosing Payment in Full to Collection Agency

1234, Main Street
Bangalore
04 April, 2008

Re: Collections Account No 1245778

Dear Sir/Madam,

Enclosed please find my cheque number 25789 in the amount of Rs.60,000 representing payment in full on the above-referenced account. I would appreciate receiving a receipt or letter from you indicating that this debt has now been satisfied and no further payments are due.

I would also request that you update my credit report with the information that this account has been closed and paid in full.

Thank you for your assistance in this matter. I look forward to hearing from you.

Regards,

Dinesh Chandra

Notice for Payment is Due Immediately

1234, Main Street
Bangalore
04 April, 2008

Re: Account No. 4578912

Dear Sir/Madam,

Please be advised that this account is now 10 days past due. Please remit a payment of Rs. 10,000 immediately to prevent this account from becoming delinquent. If we have not received payment from you within 7 days from the date of this notice, we will be forced to pursue other means of collecting on this debt.

If there is some reason why you are unable to make a payment at this time, please contact us immediately so that a payment schedule or other arrangement can be made.

Thank you for your immediate attention to this request.

Regards,

Lalit Kumar

Notification of Inability to make Regular Payment

1234, Main Street
Bangalore
04 April, 2008

Re: Account No 587496

Dear Sir/Madam,

Please be advised that due to some unavoidable circumstances, I will be unable to make this month's regular payment of Rs. 8,000.

I am enclosing a partial payment of Rs. 1,000 at this time as a symbol of my good faith.

I expect to be able to make a double payment next month, which should bring my account current.

I would appreciate it if you would contact me so we can work out a payment plan to bring my account current. I anticipate being able to resume making my regular payment by next week.

I would ask that you please not place any negative reports on my credit rating at this time. Thank you for your understanding and forbearance at this time. If you have any questions about this situation, please do not hesitate to contact me.

Regards,

Dinesh Chandra

Warning of Repossession

1234, Main Street
Bangalore
04 April, 2008

Re: Account No. 123456

Dear Sir/Madam,

Please be advised that due to the delinquent status of the above-referenced account, we will be forced to repossess the items which was financed under this account.

While we would much prefer to simply receive payment from you, your lack of payment leaves us no choice but to pursue repossession.

If you would like to avoid the embarrassment and hassle of repossession and a subsequent negative report on your credit rating, please contact us immediately or mail a payment in the amount of Rs. 30,000. If we have not heard from you within 7 days from the date of this notice, we will have no choice but to order the repossession of the items.

We hope to hear from you soon.

Regards,

Dinesh Chandra

Offer of Partial Payment as Payment in Full

1234, Main Street
Bangalore
04 April, 2008

Re: Account No. 123456

Dear Sir/Madam,

Concerning the outstanding balance on the above-referenced account, I would like to make an offer of partial payment to be accepted as payment in full. I understand the full amount of the debt is currently Rs. 1,00,000. I would be willing to make a lump sum payment of Rs.75,000 to satisfy this delinquent debt.

Please advise if this arrangement is acceptable to you. I look forward to hearing from you.

Regards,

Lalit Kumar

Polite Reminder of Due Payment

1234, Main Street
Bangalore
04 April, 2008

Re: Account No. 154789

Dear Sir/Madam,

Please be advised that the above-referenced account is now past due. Your payment of Rs. 25,000 was due on 27th of last month. To date, this amount has not yet been received. If payment has recently been made, please accept our thanks and disregard this notice. If payment has not yet been made, however, please take a moment now to send your payment and prevent this account from becoming delinquent.

Thank you for your prompt attention to this reminder.

Regards,

Dinesh Chandra

Request for Payment Plan

1234, Main Street
Bangalore
04 April, 2008

Re: Account No. 254789

Dear Sir/Madam,

I understand that the above-referenced account is delinquent. I am writing to let you know that I have every intention of repaying this debt and would appreciate it if we could work out a payment plan which will bring this account current. Please contact me at your earliest convenience to make arrangements for a payment plan. I can be reached at my phone number 2547812.

Thank you for your understanding and assistance in this matter.

Regards,

Lalit Kumar

Warning of Negative Report of Credit Rating

1234, Main Street
Bangalore
04 April, 2008

Re: Account No. 123456

Dear Sir/Madam,

Please be advised that the above-referenced account is now 7 days past due. Despite repeated requests for payment, we have not heard from you. Therefore, we are writing to inform you that if payment of the past due amount is not received within 7 days of the date of this notice, a negative report will be made to the credit agency indicating that this account has become delinquent.

In order to protect your good credit rating, please mail your payment immediately. If you are unable to make payment at this time, please notify us so that a payment schedule or other arrangement can be made.

Thank you for your immediate attention to this situation. We look forward to hearing from you.

Regards,

Dinesh Chandra

Warning that Account will be sent to Collection

1234, Main Street
Bangalore
04 April, 2005

Re: Account No. 123456

Dear Sir/Madam,

Please be advised that the above-referenced account is now 2 days past due. Despite repeated requests for payment, we have not heard from you or received payment. Accordingly, unless we hear from you or receive payment of Rs. 25,000 within 7 days from the date of this notice, we will be forced to turn this account over to a collection agency.

Please protect your credit rating and avoid the unpleasantness of dealing with a collection agency by mailing your payment or contacting us today.

Thank you for your immediate attention to this request.

Regards,

Vikas Gupta

■

16

Bank, Insurance and Mortgage Letters

Complaint of Rude Treatment by Bank Official

ABC Bank
12th Street,
Chennai
04 April, 2008

Dear Sir/Madam,

The unfortunate purpose of this letter is to complain about the rude treatment I received while conducting business on 3rd March, 2008 by one of your employee named Harish Kumar. While I am not usually one to complain, I found this behavior exceedingly unprofessional and knew that you would want to know about it so you could do something to rectify the problem.

I have been a customer at your bank since 1995 and have always been satisfied with the service I have received there. I am hopeful that this incident was a "fluke" and that it won't happen again.

Thank you for your time and consideration of this matter.

Regards,

Lalit Kumar

Complaint ATM is Often out of Order

ABC Bank
12th Street, Chennai
04 April, 2008

Dear Sir/Madam,

I am writing to complain that your ATMs are often out of service. It is such an inconvenience to make a trip to the ATM only to find it not working. I would suggest that you try to have your ATMs serviced more regularly so that they can spend more time serving your customers rather than being out of order.

I hope you will take this complaint to heart. I am sure that I am not the only one of your customers who has been inconvenienced by the unreliability of your ATMs.

Regards,

Karan Kumar

Complaint for Long Lines at Bank

ABC Bank
12th Street, Chennai
04 April, 2008

Dear Sir/Madam,

The past several times I have come into the bank to conduct business, I have been dismayed to find the line for the teller windows ridiculously long. It has not been unusual for me to have to wait in line for such a long time. Since, ultimately, yours is a service industry, I am sure you would agree that making your customers wait over tolerable time is not the best way to meet their needs.

I would suggest that you take a look at this situation and see what you can do about shortening the wait time in the teller line. I am sure all your customers would appreciate any efforts on your part to improve the service at your bank. Thank you.

Regards,

Deepesh Kumar

Letter Requesting Reconsideration of Denial of Credit

ABC Ltd.
12th Street,
Chennai
04 April, 2008

Dear Sir/Madam,

My application for a line of credit was recently denied on the basis of my credit report. Since the denial, I have received a copy of my credit report and have identified several items which were incorrect.

I have brought some problems to the attention of the credit reporting agency and they have since been deleted from my credit report.

I am, therefore, writing to ask that you reconsider my credit application in light of my improved credit report. If there is any additional information you need from me at this time, please feel free to contact me. I look forward to hearing from you.

Regards,

Lalit Kumar

Notice of Change of Address

ABC Bank
12th Street,
Chennai
04 April, 2008

Re: Change of Address
Account Number 25489

Dear Sir/Madam,

Please be advised that, effective from the above mentioned date, my address will change. My new address and phone number will be:

D-21, F Block, Vikaspuri, New Delhi

New telephone number is 254789

Please update my account with the above information. Thank you for your assistance. If you have any questions, please do not hesitate to contact me.

Regards,

Manoj Kumar

Notice to Bank of Erroneously Bounced Cheques

ABC Bank
12th Street,
Chennai
04 April, 2008

Re: Account No. 244587

Dear Sir/Madam,

On 2nd of April, I received a notice that my cheque numbered 145789 had been returned due to non-sufficient funds. After a careful review of my records, I have determined that indeed there were sufficient funds in my account to cover this cheque, and that it was a mistake on your part that caused it to be returned.

I would, therefore, ask that you please reverse any and all service charges that have been applied to my account due to the returned cheque. I would also ask that you accept this cheque when they are presented for payment and that you reimburse me for fees charged by the merchants to whom it was written.

Because the fault is yours, I think this is the least you can do to correct the situation. While I realize that we all make mistakes, I certainly hope that you will be careful not to allow this to happen again in the future.

Thank you for your immediate attention to this situation.

Regards,

Jagdish Chandra

Request for Copy of Statement

ABC Bank
12th Street,
Chennai
04 April, 2008

Re: Request for Copy of Statement
Account No. 25478

Dear Sir/Madam,

In searching through my files, I am unable to locate my March, 2005 statement on the above-referenced account. I would, therefore, appreciate it if you would please send a copy of this statement to the address herein.

Thank you for your prompt attention to this request. If you have any questions, please do not hesitate to contact me.

Regards,

Lalit Kumar

Request for Copy of Cancelled Cheque

ABC Bank
12th Street,
Chennai
04 April, 2008

Re: Request for Copy of Cheque
Account No. 25489

Dear Sir/Madam,

I would appreciate it if you would please provide me with a copy of a canceled cheque on this account. I am interested in cheque number 25489, which was made payable on 30th of March,

2008 in the amount of Rs. 25,000. Please make sure that the copy you provide shows both the front and back of the canceled cheque.

Thank you for your prompt attention to this request. If you have any questions, please do not hesitate to contact me.

Regards,

Lalit Kumar

Request for Interest Rate Information

ABC Bank
12th Street,
Chennai
04 April, 2005

Re: Interest Rates

Dear Sir/Madam,

I would appreciate it if you would please send me information concerning the interest rates currently being earned by your account.

Please also let me know whether or not a minimum balance must be kept in order to qualify for that particular interest rate, as well as if there are any time period requirements on how long my money must stay in the account for it to earn interest at that rate.

Thank you for your attention to this request.

Please mail the information to the address herein, or fax it to me at 25478. I look forward to hearing from you.

Regards,

Manoj Kumar

Request for Loan Information

ABC Bank
12th Street, Chennai
04 April, 2005

Re: New Loan

Dear Sir/Madam,

I am interested in applying for a home loan with your bank. I would appreciate if you would please send me an application, as well as any brochures or pamphlets which you have regarding this type of loan. I would also like to know what interest rate you are currently charging on this particular loan.

Thank you for your attention to this request. Please mail this information to me at the address herein, or you may fax it to me at 24578. I look forward to hearing from you.

Regards,

Lalit Kumar

Request for Bank Card Replacement

ABC Bank
12th Street, Chennai
04 April, 2008

Re: Account No. 21457

Dear Sir/Madam,

I recently lost or misplaced my bank card on the above-referenced account. The lost card bore the number 365478954. I am writing to ask that you cancel that card and issue me a replacement card as soon as possible. No further use of this card should be authorized under any circumstances.

I appreciate your prompt attention to this request. If you have any questions concerning this, please do not hesitate to contact me.

Regards,

Lalit Kumar

Request to Close Account

ABC Bank
12th Street,
Chennai
04 April, 2008

Re: Closure of Account
Account No. 214578

Dear Sir/Madam,

Please be advised that I wish to close the above-referenced savings account with your institution. I believe the balance of this account is Rs. 12,000. I would appreciate it if you would please close the account and send me a cashier's cheque in this amount, minus any applicable service fees. The closing paperwork and cashier's cheque may be sent to me at my address.

Thank you for your attention to this request. If you have any questions, please feel free to contact me.

Regards,

Manish Mathur

Request to Stop Payment on Cheque

ABC Bank
12th Street,
Chennai
04 April, 2008

Re: Request for Stop Payment
Account No. 2547789

Dear Sir/Madam,

I am writing to request that you stop payment on a cheque written on the above-referenced account. I would like to stop payment on cheque number 21456, which was issued on 2nd of April, 2008 and made payable to Mr. Sumit Kumar. The cheque was issued in the amount of Rs. 25,000. I would appreciate it if you would provide me with written confirmation that payment on this cheque has been stopped. Thank you for your assistance in this matter.

Regards,

Amit Negi

Request to Transfer Funds between Accounts

ABC Bank
12th Street,
Chennai
04 April, 2008

Dear Sir/Madam,

I am writing to request a transfer of funds between accounts. Please transfer Rs. 10,000 from my savings account, number. 214587, to my current account, number 2589784. I would appreciate being provided a receipt for this transaction.

Thank you for your assistance. If you have any questions, please feel free to contact me.

Regards,

Abhimanyu Sanjay

Letter to Health Agent in Lienholder

XYZ Insurance
Dalal street,
Mumbai
05 April, 2008

Re: Policy No. 25478

Dear Sir/Madam,

Please be advised that I have recently refinanced my insured property covered by this policy. The new lienholder is Mr. Shashikant Jha and the new account number is 54789. If you need any further information to update your files, please feel free to contact me or Mr. Jha at your convenience.

Thank you for your continued assistance.

Regards,

Manish Dubey

Notification of Claim Auto Accident

ABC Insurance
Dalal Street,
Mumbai
05 April, 2008

Re: Policy No. 54789

Dear Sir/Madam,

Please be advised that I would like to make a claim on the above-referenced policy of insurance. On 27th of March, 2005 I was in an automobile accident at my neighbourhood place in Delhi. <Name of insured> insured as follows:

Name of driver — Sudhir Kumar

Name of their insurer — XYZ insurance

Their policy number — 54789

A police report was obtained at the time of the accident. The report is number 25467 and can be obtained through the agency.

I would, therefore, request to adjust any claims arising out of this accident. Please contact me if you need any additional information. I look forward to hearing from you.

Regards,

Pawan Kumar

Letter to Health Insurance Enclosing Completed Claims Forms

XYZ Insurance
Dalal Street, Mumbai
05 April, 2008

Re: Member No. 25687

Group No. 14589

Dear Sir/Madam,

Enclosed please find three completed claim forms regarding the above-referenced health insurance policy. I would appreciate it if you would please process these claims immediately and forward drafts to the provider.

If you have any questions about any of these claims, please do not hesitate to contact me. Thank you for your assistance in this matter.

Regards,

Manoj Kumar

Letter to Health Insurance Requesting Claim Forms

XYZ Insurance
Dalal Street, Mumbai
05 April, 2008

Re: Member No. 32564

Group No. 5689

Dear Sir/Madam,

I would appreciate it if you could please send me three claim forms for use in reporting claims on the above-referenced health insurance policy.

Thank you for your assistance.

Regards,

Lalit Kumar

Letter to Health Insurance Requesting Reimbursement of Costs

XYZ Insurance
Dalal street, Mumbai
05 April, 2008

Re: Member No. 54887
Group No. 3654

Dear Sir/Madam,

Enclosed please find receipts for some of the undesired expenses. I would appreciate it if you would please send me a cheque equalling these expenses to reimburse me for these out of pocket expenses.

Thank you for your attention to this request. If you have any questions about any of these items, please do not hesitate to contact me.

Regards,

Jagdish Kumar

Notification of Claim Property Damage

XYZ Insurance
Dalal Street, Mumbai
05 April, 2008

Re: Policy No. 589785

Dear Sir/Madam,

Please be advised that I would like to make a claim on the above-referenced policy of insurance. On 30th of March, 2008, due to and accident my insured property was damaged. I would, therefore, request to pay for the repair of damaged property. Please contact me as soon as possible to arrange for the adjustment of this claim.

I look forward to hearing from you.

Regards,

Manoj Kumar

Request for Copy of Claim File

XYZ Insurance
Dalal Street,
Mumbai
05 April, 2008

Re: Policy No. 54789

Dear Sir/Madam,

I would appreciate it if you would provide me with a copy of the file on claim number 2145 covered under the above-referenced insurance policy.

Thank you for your prompt attention to this request. I look forward to hearing from you.

Regards,

Lalit Kumar

Request for Copy of Policy

XYZ Insurance
Dalal Street,
Mumbai
05 April, 2008

Re: Policy No 12345678

Dear Sir/Madam,

I would appreciate if you would please forward to me a copy of the above-referenced insurance policy on my insured asset. Thank you for your prompt attention to this request.

Regards,

Lalit Kumar

Request for Insurance Rate Quotation

XYZ Insurance
Dalal Street,
Mumbai
05 April, 2008

Dear Sir/Madam,

I am interested in obtaining a policy of insurance for my property to insure. If you should need more information regarding my property to insure, please advise, or simply send me an application.

Thank you for your attention to this request. I look forward to hearing from you.

Regards,

Manoj Kumar

Request for Reimbursement Under Policy

XYZ Insurance
Dalal Street,
Mumbai
05 April, 2008

Re: Policy No. 658974

Dear Sir/Madam,

On 20th of March, 2005, I paid Rs. 10,000 to repair my property which is insured by your company. Because this expenditure was the result of a covered loss under my policy of insurance with XYZ insurance, I would appreciate it if you would reimburse me for this amount as soon as possible.

If you have any questions about this request, please feel free to contact me. I look forward to hearing from you.

Regards,

Pawan Kumar

Request to Add New Car to Policy

XYZ Insurance
Dalal Street, Mumbai
05 April, 2008

Re: Policy No. 54689

Dear Sir/Madam,

Please be advised that I have recently purchased a new car which I would like to add to my existing policy of insurance. My new car is a 2008 model. The details regarding model name, car no. and other related information on my car has been given in a separate attached copy. Please see that this vehicle is added to my policy as soon as possible.

If you have any questions or need further information, please do not hesitate to contact me.

Regards,

Dhiraj Kumar

Request to Cancel Policy

XYZ Insurance
Dalal Street, Mumbai
05 April, 2008

Re: Policy No. 25478

Dear Sir/Madam,

Please be advised that I wish to cancel the above-referenced insurance policy with XYZ Insurance. Please cancel the policy immediately. Please forward any premium refund to me at my address which is the same as in this policy.

Thank you for your prompt attention to this request. I would appreciate receiving written confirmation that this policy has been closed. I look forward to hearing from you.

Regards,

Lalit Kumar

Request to Change Policy Beneficiary

XYZ Insurance
Dalal Street, Mumbai
05 April, 2008

Re: Policy No. 5478925

Dear Sir/Madam,

With regard to the above-referenced policy of insurance, I would like to change the beneficiary information. Instead of current beneficiary, I would like to name Mr. Deepak Kapoor and Mr. Suresh Kumar as the co-beneficiary of this policy.

Thank you for your attention to this request. If you have any questions concerning this change, please do not hesitate to contact me.

Regards,

Pawan Kumar

Request to Change Policy Limits

XYZ Insurance
Dalal Street, Mumbai
05 April, 2008

Re: Policy No. 547892

Dear Sir/Madam,

I believe that, currently, my insurance policy bears limits of 2,00,000. After careful consideration, I have decided that I would like to raise my policy limits. I would like my new limits to be 4,00,000. I would appreciate if you could effect this change as soon as possible.

If you have any questions or need further information, please do not hesitate to contact me.

Regards,

Lalit Kumar

Tender of Defence of Lawsuit

XYZ Insurance
Dalal Street, Mumbai
05 April, 2008

Re: Policy No. 547895
Case No. 0245486

Dear Sir/Madam,

On 22nd of March, I was served with a Summons and Complaint in the above-referenced matter. Copies of these documents are enclosed for your review. As you will see from a review of the documents, this matter stems from the incident which prompted the lawsuit and that incident I have mentioned for your review.

It is my understanding that my policy of insurance should cover such an incident, and therefore, XYZ Insurance is obligated to defend me in this matter. Accordingly, I hereby tender my defense in the above-referenced matter to XYZ insurance.

Please advise if I should select my own attorney or if you will be appointing one to my case. I look forward to hearing from you on this matter.

Regards,

Kavita Nagpal

Letter Requesting Application for New Mortgage Loan

ABC Bank
Dalal Street,
Mumbai
05 April, 2008

Dear Sir/Madam,

I am interested in applying for a mortgage loan with ABC Bank. I would appreciate it if you would please send me information on your mortgage loans, including current interest rates, minimum amount of down payment you require, etc. I would also appreciate being provided an application form. You may mail the information to me at my address, C-45, Sunder Nagar, New Delhi.

Thank you for your attention to this request. I look forward to hearing from you.

Regards,

Pawan Kumar

Letter Requesting Service under Home Warranty Plan

1234, Main Street
Chennai
05 April, 2005

Re: Home Warranty No. 25489

Dear Sir/Madam,

I need certain items in my home, which is covered under the home warranty referenced above. The list of item has been attached separately. Please send one of your service technicians out as soon as possible to either repair or replace the items in need of work.

I look forward to hearing from you shortly.

Regards,

Mahendra Rawat

Letter to Mortgage Company Payment Problem

ABC Bank
Dalal Street, Mumbai
05 April, 2008

Re: Mortgage Loan No. 214578

Dear Sir/Madam,

With regard to the above-referenced mortgage loan, please be advised that, due to some reason,

I am experiencing some financial difficulties. It will not be possible for me to make my mortgage payment for the month of April, 2008.

I am enclosing a partial payment of Rs. 5,000 at this time as a symbol of my good faith.

I anticipate being able to resume making my regular payment by next month.

I would certainly appreciate it if you would contact me so that we can work out a payment plan which will allow me to bring my account current and prevent a default on this mortgage loan. I want to do everything I can to avoid a foreclosure. Thank you for your assistance and forbearance during this difficult time. I look forward to hearing from you.

Regards,

Sumit Narayan

Request to Add New Spouse to New Mortgage Loan

ABC Bank,
Dalal Street,
Mumbai
05 April, 2008

Re: Mortgage Loan No 214598

Dear Sir/Madam,

Please be advised that I have recently married. My new wife and I are making our home at the property financed by the above-referenced loan. I am interested in adding my wife's name to the title and loan for this property and would appreciate if you would send me any documents and/ or applications which need to be processed in order to make this change.

Thank you for your attention to this request. I look forward to hearing from you.

Regards,

Pawan Kumar

Letter to Loan Officer Enclosing Requested Documents

ABC Bank
Dalal Street, Mumbai
05 April, 2008

Dear Sir/Madam,

Pursuant to your request, enclosed please find the following documents:

- <list of documents>

Thank you for your continued assistance in processing my loan application. If there is anything else you need, please do not hesitate to call.

Regards,

Lalit Kumar

Letter to Mortgage Company Requesting Information on Existing Loan

ABC Bank
Dalal Street,
Mumbai
05 April, 2008

Re: Mortgage Loan No. 25468

Dear Sir/Madam,

I would appreciate if you could please provide me information on the above-referenced loan. Please send this information as soon as possible at my address, C-45, Sunder Nagar, New Delhi.

Thank you for your attention to this request.

Regards,

Lalit Kumar

Notice on Change of Name

ABC Bank
Dalal Street, Mumbai
05 April, 2008

Re: Mortgage Account No. 124578

Dear Sir/Madam,

Please be advised that I have recently married and taken my husband's name and legally changed my name. My new name is Sunita Verma. I would appreciate if you would please update your records on the above-referenced account to reflect this change.

Thank you for your attention to this request.

Regards,

Sunita Verma

Request for Reimbursement Under Home Warranty Policy

1234, Main Street, Chennai
05 April, 2008

Re: Home Warranty No. 145678

Dear Sir/Madam,

Please be advised that I have had to replace the item in my home, which was covered under the above-referenced policy. The cost for this came to Rs. 10,000. I have enclosed a copy of the receipt for this for your reference. I would appreciate if you would forward a cheque to me in that amount as reimbursement for this item.

If you have any questions about this, please do not hesitate to contact me.

Regards,

Lalit Kumar

■

17

Property Letters

Letter to Former Landlord Requesting Referral Letter

1234, Main Street
New Delhi
05 April, 2008

Hello,

As you know, I was your tenant from November 2006 to March 2008. During that time, I paid my rent in a consistent and timely fashion. I was wondering if you would consider providing me with a letter of reference which I may present to any prospective landlords, indicating that I am a good tenant and that you were happy with my payment habits and the condition of the property when I left.

Thank you for your assistance and consideration of this request. The referral letter may be sent to me at C-45, Sunder Nagar, New Delhi.

If you have any questions, please do not hesitate to contact me.

Regards,

Lalit Kumar

Bill to Former Tenant for Cleaning or Repairs

1234, Main Street
New Delhi
05 April, 2008

Hello,

Please be advised that, due to the poor condition in which you left the property, I am unable to refund any of your security/cleaning deposit. In fact, the property was left in such a state that I have had to spend more than the security/cleaning deposit to restore it to its previous condition.

According to our Rental Agreement, I am entitled to bill you for the cost of cleaning and/or repairs over and above the amount of the security deposit. Therefore, please forward to me a cheque in the amount of Rs.10,000 to cover the additional costs of cleaning and repairing the rental.

Thank you for your immediate attention to this request.

Regards,

Pawankant Singh

Letter to Former Tenant Enclosing Refund of Security Deposit

25/46, Main Street
Bangalore
05 April, 2008

Hello,

Enclosed please find my cheque number 25468 in the amount of Rs. 10,000 representing a partial refund of your security/cleaning deposit. I certainly appreciate the clean and tidy condition in which you left the property. Required repairs and cleaning were required, costing Rs. 5,000 and preventing me from being able to refund the full amount of your deposit. If you have questions about the repairs or cleaning, please contact me at 235468.

I wish you best of luck in the future.

Regards,

Lalit Kumar

Letter to Landlord for Payment Problem

25/46, Main Street
Bangalore
05 April, 2008

Hello,

I am writing to let you know that, due to some reasons, I am experiencing some financial difficulties. It will not be possible for me to make my rent payment for the month of April, 2008.

I am enclosing a partial payment of Rs. 2,000 at this time as a symbol of my good faith. I anticipate being able to resume making my regular payment by next month. I would certainly appreciate if you would contact me so that we can work out a payment plan which will allow me to bring the rent current and prevent further arrears. I want to do everything I can to avoid having to move out. Thank you for your assistance and forbearance during this difficult time. I look forward to hearing from you.

Regards,

Hem Verma

Letter to Landlord Requesting Reimbursement for Repair made

25/46, Main Street
Bangalore
05 April, 2008

Hello,

Please be advised that I was able to perform the repairs you authorized. I believe the repairs were made in a professional and workmanlike manner. In carrying out the repairs, I had to purchase a number of supplies and materials, the list of which I have enclosed separately. I have attached my receipts for these items and would appreciate if you would please send me a cheque in the amount of Rs. 5,000 as reimbursement for these costs. If you prefer, I would be happy to simply deduct this amount from my next month's rent.

Please let me know how you wish to handle the reimbursement for the cost of the repairs I made. I look forward to hearing from you.

Regards,

Lalit Kumar

Letter to Landlord Requesting Repairs

25/46, Main Street
Bangalore
05 April, 2008

Hello,

Please be advised that the following repair needs to be made at the property:

- <list of repairs>

I am willing and able to make these repairs myself, but would like your authorisation to proceed with the repairs, as well as your agreement to reimburse me for any materials and supplies I may need to purchase to perform the repairs.

If you intend to hire a contractor/repair person to carry out the requested repairs, I would appreciate if you would notify me of the date and time when I might expect that person to be on the premises.

Thank you for your prompt attention to this request.

Regards,

Lalit Kumar

Letter to Landlord not Happy about Raise in Rent

25/46, Main Street
Bangalore
05 April, 2008

Hello,

I am in receipt of your notice of 28th of March, 2008, indicating that the rent on the property will be raised to Rs. 10,000 as of 1st May, 2008. I am writing to express my disappointment at this raise in the rent and to ask that you reconsider such an action.

I have been a tenant at this property for the last four years. In that time, I have paid my rent in a consistent and timely fashion. While I do not relish the idea of having to move, the increase in rent will be a hardship for me and may, ultimately, force me to look for rental property elsewhere.

Thank you for your consideration of this request. I hope to hear from you soon.

Regards,

Lalit Kumar

Letter to Prospective Landlord Confirming Move in Date and Terms

25/46, Main Street
Bangalore
05 April, 2008

Hello,

This letter will confirm that, according to our lease agreement, I will be moving into the property on 10th of April, 2008.

Please let me know when I may pick up the keys to the property. I will want to have the utilities turned on by 7th of April and will need the keys on or before that time.

Thank you for your assistance. I look forward to hearing from you.

Regards,

Pawan Kumar

Letter to Prospective Tenant Confirming Move in Date and Terms

25/46, Main Street
Bangalore
05 April, 2008

Hello,

This letter will confirm that, according to the lease agreement entered into between us, you will be moving into the property on 10th of April, 2008.

In order to prepare the property for your occupancy, I have agreed to some repairs in this property.

You may pick up the keys to the property from me. If you have any questions or concerns about the property, please do not hesitate to contact me. I look forward to working with you and hope that you will be happy in your new home.

Regards,

Ramesh Singh

Letter of Tenant Confirming About Move out Date and Terms

25/46, Main Street
Bangalore
05 April, 2008

Hello,

This will confirm that you have given me your notice of intent to vacate the property. Your anticipated move-out date is 20th April, 2008.

Because you will be moving out during the middle of the month, your final month's rent will be prorated accordingly.

As you know, you gave me a cleaning and security deposit of Rs. 5000 at the time when you moved in. The condition in which you leave the property will dictate how much of that amount I am able to return to you. Please give me your forwarding address so that I may send any refund of this deposit to you.

If there are any repairs to the property which need to be made, I would appreciate if you would let me know immediately.

Regards,

Lalit Kumar

Notice to Tenant Lowering Rent

25/46, Main Street
Bangalore
05 April, 2008

Hello,

Please be advised that, in order to remain competitive with rents in the area, I have decided to lower the rent on the property. Currently, the monthly rent is Rs. 6000. As of next month, the rent will be Rs. 5500.

I appreciate your tenancy and hope that the property continues to meet your needs. Please let me know if you have any questions or problems with the property.

Regards,

Jitendra Prashad

Referral Letter for Former Tenant

25/46, Main Street
Bangalore
05 April, 2008

Hello,

The purpose of this letter is to recommend Mr. Upadhyay as a tenant. Mr. Upadhyay rented property from me from November, 2002 until March, 2008. During that time, he consistently paid the rent in a timely fashion and took excellent care of the property. Whenever he had any problems or if repairs were needed, he notified me right away and were very cooperative in scheduling the repairs to be done.

Mr. Upadhyay was an excellent tenant and a pleasure to know. I certainly would recommend him highly as a tenant.

Regards,

Lalit Kumar

Notice to Tenant Raising Rent

25/46, Main Street
Bangalore
05 April, 2008

Hello,

Please be advised that, in order to remain consistent with rents in the area and to keep up with increasing costs of maintenance, it has become necessary to raise the rent on the property. Currently, the monthly rent is Rs. 5000. As of next month, the rent will be Rs. 6000.

I appreciate your continued tenancy and hope that this property is meeting your needs. If you have any questions or problems with the property, please do not hesitate to contact me.

Regards,

Lalit Kumar

■

(18)

Donation and Money Related Letters

Cash Donation to a Charity

25/46, Main Street
Bangalore
05 April, 2008

Dear Sir/Madam,

Because I respect the fine work that your organisation does and want to help ensure that work may continue, I would like to offer a donation at this time. Accordingly, please find enclosed my cheque in the amount of Rs. 10,000, made payable to your organisation. I would appreciate if you would please provide me a written receipt for this gift.

Thank you for the excellent service you provide to our community.

Regards,

Dhiraj Kumar

Letter Acknowledging Donation

25/46, Main Street
Bangalore
05 April, 2008

Dear Sir/Madam,

Thank you so much for your recent donation of Rs. 10,000. Please consider this letter your receipt.

As you know, charity could not exist were it not for the generosity of people such as yourself. Thanks to you, we can continue to serve the community through charity work. It's people like you who truly make a difference and make community name a better place to live.

Thank you once again for your generosity and support.

Regards,

Sushil Harsh

Non Cash Donation to Charity

25/46, Main Street
Bangalore
05 April, 2008

Dear Sir/Madam,

Because I admire the fine work your organisation does in our community, I would like to offer you a donation at this time. I have a property to donote which I think might be of benefit to you. If you are interested in accepting this donation, please contact me at 24564852 to arrange a pick up day and time. I would appreciate it if, at the time of the pick up, you would please provide me with a receipt for this item.

Thank you for the excellent service you provide to our community. I look forward to hearing from you.

Regards,

Lalit Kumar

Soliciting a New Donation

25/46, Main Street
Bangalore
05 April, 2008

Dear Sir/Madam,

I am writing to acquaint you with <name of charity> and some of the work that we do right here in your community. For the past <number of years>, our organisation has been involved in

<nature of charitable work>. All of us involved with <name of charity> find this work both rewarding and gratifying.

As I am sure you know, however, funding for organisations like ours must come from the community we serve. Therefore, if you believe that what we are doing is important and enriches your community, I would ask that you consider providing us with a donation to help make sure this important work can continue. We don't ask for a particular amount, only that you give what you can — whatever you feel comfortable with.

I thank you for your attention to this request and your willingness to help make a difference. If you have any questions about <name of charity> we would be only too happy to answer them for you. Please do not hesitate to contact us.

Regards,

Lalit Kumar

Soliciting Donations from Existing Donors

25/46, Main Street
Bangalore
05 April, 2008

Dear Sir/Madam,

I would like to thank you for your generous support of <name of charity>. Your donation has made our continuing work possible. This year, we have been fortunate to have accomplished so much. None of this would have been possible without your support.

That is why we again turn to you for help. We would be grateful if you would once more consider donating what you can to this important cause. Your support has really helped make a difference in our community, and we would like to see that support continue.

Please donate whatever you can afford and know that you have our heartfelt thanks. <name of charity> could not reach its goals without the backing of prominent, generous members of the community such as yourself.

Regards,

Lalit Kumar

Business Letters to Creditors Advising them about Bankruptcy

25/46, Main Street
Bangalore
05 April, 2008

Dear Sir/Madam,

Re: Account No. 21458

Please be advised that, due to insurmountable financial difficulties, our company has been forced to declare bankruptcy. With the help of our attorney, we have begun Chapter proceedings. All of company's debts will be turned over to a trustee in bankruptcy who will evaluate each debt and place it in line either for payment or discharge through the bankruptcy process.

I would appreciate if you would direct any further inquiries regarding this account to our bankruptcy attorney, Mr. Goyal. He can be reached at his phone number 2568974.

The trustee in bankruptcy will be in touch with you regarding the status of your account and its standing in the bankruptcy process.

Regards,

Sumit Kumar

Letter from Executor Requesting Status of Probate

25/46, Main Street
Bangalore
05 April, 2008

Dear Sir/Madam,

It has been some time since I heard from you regarding the probate of Mr. Khanna's will. I would appreciate if you would please provide me with a brief status report regarding the progress in this matter.

Thank you for your assistance and attention to this request. I look forward to hearing from you.

Regards,

Lalit Kumar

Letter from Executor to Beneficiaries Enclosing your Request

25/46, Main Street
Bangalore
05 April, 2008

Dear Sir/Madam,

I am pleased to announce that the probate process has finally concluded and the will of <name of deceased> is now ready for execution.

Accordingly, please find enclosed a cheque made payable to you in the amount of <amount> representing the bequest left to you by <name of deceased>.

If you have any questions about this bequest, please feel free to contact me or the probate attorney. Thank you for your patience during this long process.

Regards,

Jatin Kumar

Letter to Bankruptcy Trustee Requesting Status of Case

25/46, Main Street
Bangalore
05 April, 2008

Re: Bankruptcy Case No. 25489

Dear Sir/Madam,

It has been some time since I have heard anything from you or the court regarding the above-referenced bankruptcy proceedings. I would appreciate if you would provide me with a brief status report regarding any progress that has been made in this matter.

Thank you for your attention to this request. I look forward to hearing from you.

Regards,

Lalit Kumar

Letter to Stockbroker Instructing to Buy and Sell

25/46, Main Street
Bangalore
05 April, 2008

Dear Sir/Madam,

After careful consideration, I have decided that I would like to buy 500 shares of ABC Limited. I believe the current stock price is Rs. 100 per share. I am hereby authorizing you to conduct this transaction on my behalf. I would appreciate receiving written confirmation that this purchase has been completed.

Thank you for your assistance in this matter.

Regards,

Lalit Kumar

Letter of Trustee Requesting to be Added to list of Creditors

25/46, Main Street
Bangalore
05 April, 2008

Re: Bankruptcy Case No. 24578

Dear Sir/Madam,

I understand that ABC Ltd. is insolvent and has initiated bankruptcy proceedings under the above-referenced case number. As one of its creditors, I am writing to ask that I be included on the list of creditors and that ABC Ltd.'s account with me be considered for payment through the bankruptcy process. As of the date of this letter, the total amount owed me by ABC Ltd. is Rs. 1,00,000.

I would appreciate if you would forward to me any forms which I must submit to complete this process. Thank you for your attention to this request. I look forward to hearing from you.

Regards,

Jatin Gandhi

Personal Letter to Creditors Advising them you are in Bankruptcy

25/46, Main Street
Bangalore
05 April, 2008

Re: Account No. 25478

Dear Sir/Madam,

Please be advised that, due to insurmountable financial difficulties, I have been forced to declare personal bankruptcy. All of my debts will be turned over to a trustee in bankruptcy who will evaluate each debt and place it in line either for payment or discharge through the bankruptcy process.

I would appreciate if you would direct any further inquiries regarding this account to my bankruptcy attorney, Mr. Vikas Garg. He can be reached at 254461. The trustee in bankruptcy will be in touch with you regarding the status of your account and its standing in the bankruptcy process.

Regards,

Sahil Seth

Letter of Stockbroker Requesting Current Value of Portfolio

25/46, Main Street
Bangalore
05 April, 2008

Dear Sir/Madam,

I am in the process of evaluating my current financial position and would appreciate if you would provide me with a summary of my account with you, indicating all shares held and their current values. If you feel that this would be a good time to make any changes to my portfolio, I would appreciate your input in this regard.

Thank you for your continuing assistance. I look forward to hearing from you.

Regards,

Lalit Kumar

■

(19)

Revenue Services Letters

Asking Tax Questions

25/46, Main Street
Bangalore
05 April, 2008

Dear Sir/Madam,

I was filing my income tax when I had some problems regarding filing this form. I am sending these questions in a separate attached sheet.

Please contact me with the answers as soon as possible. You may call at 2145789.

Thank you for your time and assistance.

Regards,

Lalit Kumar

Arranging Tax Payment Plan

25/46, Main Street
Bangalore
05 April, 2008

Dear Sir/Madam,

I was shocked to see that my income tax debt for the tax year 2004 came out to a total of Rs. 50,000. With my normal expenses, I cannot hope to pay this entire tax debt in a single payment. Therefore, I am writing to inquire if a payment plan can be arranged to pay off this debt. This plan would get the debt paid while allowing me to avoid an unbearable financial burden.

Please contact me with your approval of this plan, or to discuss the details.

Thank you for your understanding.

Regards,

Pawan Kumar

Disputing Tax Bills

25/46, Main Street
Bangalore
05 April, 2008

Dear Sir/Madam,

When I hired tax preparer to prepare my taxes, I trusted that the result would be correct. Unfortunately, that has not proven to be the case. The result of my tax preparation stated that I owe Rs. 50,000. This is clearly in error and I have no intention of paying that amount.

I would like to discuss this matter with a representative to see if we can reach an acceptable solution. It may be that I will need to have my taxes computed by the representative, and if that is the case the necessary documents and receipts can be provided.

This is a grave error that must be corrected. Please have someone contact <me/us> as soon as possible to discuss the matter.

Thank you for your time.

Regards,

Lalit Kumar

Claiming Exemptions

25/46, Main Street
Bangalore
05 April, 2008

Dear Sir/Madam,

I assert that I am exempt from paying federal income tax for <year>, because <reason>.

If there is some error in this statement of exemption, please notify me of it immediately. Thank you.

Regards,

Lalit Kumar

Filing by Internet

25/46, Main Street
Bangalore
05 April, 2008

Dear Sir/Madam,

<I/We> would like to file <my/our> income tax via the Internet this year. However, having never used this filing method before, <I/We> have some questions.

Must <I/We> get on the World Wide Web, or is there a proprietary online system that must be used? If the Web is used, what is the site address? Is there a charge? Do <I/We> need any special information?

Please contact <me/us> with the appropriate information as soon as possible. You may call at <phone number>, write to <address>, or send e-mail to <e-mail address>

Thank you for your time and assistance.

Regards,

Lalit Kumar

Filing by Phone

25/46, Main Street
Bangalore
05 April, 2008

Dear Sir/Madam,

I would like to file my income tax by phone this year. However, having never used this filing method before, I have some questions. What number do I call? Are there specific calling hours? Is there any charge? Do I need any additional material besides the tax return form?

Please contact me with the appropriate information as soon as possible. You may call at my phone number 245789.

Thank you for your time and assistance.

Regards,

Lalit Kumar

Late Tax Payment

25/46, Main Street, Bangalore
05 April, 2008

Dear Sir/Madam,

As you can see by this envelope's postmark, I am <time you are late> late in sending in my <year> tax return. I understand that there will be some penalties for late filing, but I thought it important to inform you that my return is late.

I believe this constitutes a valid reason for filing my return late, and I hope you will see your way clear to waive the interest charges and/or penalties involved. Please have an IRS representative contact me to discuss this matter.

Thank you.

Regards,

Lalit Kumar

Overpaid Taxes

25/46, Main Street, Bangalore
05 April, 2008

Dear Sir/Madam,

For the tax year 2007, I have discovered that I overpaid my income tax. I paid Rs. 50,000 while upon further calculation I should have only paid Rs. 30,000 . I believe this overpayment entitles me to a refund of the difference, Rs. 20,000.

Please contact <me/us> if there are any questions about this overpayment or the specified refund. If there are no questions, please forward a refund cheque to <me/us> as soon as possible.

Thank you.

Regards,

Lalit Kumar

Request to Change Audit Date

25/46, Main Street, Bangalore
05 April, 2008

Dear Sir/Madam,

Currently, <I/We> have a tax audit scheduled for <date>. Unfortunately, circumstances have made it impossible for <me/us> to meet the IRS requirements for the audit by that date. <I/We> <am/are> writing in the hopes that the date can be changed.

If possible, <I/We> would like the audit moved back to <date> or later. This would give <me/us> sufficient time to prepare. Please contact <me/us> to confirm this arrangement or if there is a problem. Thank you for your understanding.

Regards,

Pawan Kumar

Underpaid Taxes

25/46, Main Street, Bangalore
05 April, 2008

Dear Sir/Madam,

For the tax year <year>, <I/we> have discovered that <I/we> underpaid <my/our> income tax. <I/we> paid <amount>, while upon further calculation <I/we> should have paid <amount>. <I/we> believe this underpayment means <I/we> owe the <state/government> a balance of <amount>, plus an interest and penalties.

Please contact <me/us> as soon as possible to let <me/us> know about any interest or penalties that may be applicable.

Thank you for your time.

Regards,

Dhiraj Joshi

■

20

Attorney and Contract Letters

Letter Referring to Another Party to your Attorney

25/46, Main Street
Bangalore
06 April, 2008

Re: Income tax settlement case

Dear Sir/Madam,

Please be advised that I have retained an attorney to represent me in the above-referenced matter. In the future, please address all correspondence, inquiries or demands to my attorney, Mr. Harsh Gupta.

Regards,

Lalit Kumar

Letter to Attorney Confirming Retention

25/46, Main Street
Bangalore
06 April, 2008

Re: Income tax settlement case

Dear Sir/Madam,

This will confirm that you have agreed to act as my attorney in the above-referenced matter. Pursuant to our retainer agreement, you will bill me for your time at a rate of <hourly or flat fee

rate>, to be billed on a <billing interval> basis. In return, you will represent my interests in this lawsuit and work to bring about a speedy and positive conclusion of the case.

I will, of course, direct any further inquiries or correspondence I receive regarding this matter to your office. Thank you for your assistance and professional handling of this case.

I would appreciate receiving periodic reports of your progress in settling this matter. I look forward to hearing from you.

Regards,

Lalit Kumar

Letter to Attorney Requesting an Update in Your Case

25/46, Main Street
Bangalore
06 April, 2008

Re: Income Tax Case

Dear Sir/Madam,

It has been some time since I have heard from your office. I would appreciate being provided with a brief update on the status of my case.

Thank you for your continuing assistance in this matter. I look forward to hearing from you.

Regards,

Lalit Kumar

Letter to Attorney Requesting Copies of Document

25/46, Main Street
Bangalore
06 April, 2008

Re: <insert case name>

Dear Sir/Madam,

I would appreciate if you would please provide me with copies of <name of document(s)> for my records. Thank you for your assistance in this matter.

Regards,

Lalit Kumar

General Contract Addendum

25/46, Main Street
Bangalore
06 April, 2008

Dear Sir/Madam,

Use the "General Addendum", under the Subject "General Forms" as the basis of a contract addendum.

Regards,

Lalit Kumar

General Contract

25/46, Main Street
Bangalore
06 April, 2008

Dear Sir/Madam,

Use the "General Agreement", under the Subject "General Forms" as the basis for a general contract.

Regards,

Lalit Kumar

Notice of Breach of Contract

25/46, Main Street
Bangalore
06 April, 2008

Dear Sir/Madam,

You are hereby put on notice that as of now you are in breach of our contract dated 19th of May, 2007. The nature of said breach is attached in a separate copy.

It is our desire to inform you of the foregoing and afford you the opportunity to cure said breach. You may in any event be held responsible for all damages arising from said breach.

You have until 15th of April, 2009 to cure said breach, after which we will be forced to take further action.

Regards,

Pawan Singh

■

21

Buying, Selling and Claim Letters

Buyers Notice of Dissatisfaction

25/46, Third Street
Exhibition Road,
Bangalore
06 April, 2008

Dear Sir/Madam,

On 16th of March, I purchased an item of your company. Unfortunately, I am not satisfied with this product because of some technical problems. Accordingly, I would request that you to take some suitable action in this matter.

Please contact me as soon as possible to arrange for this solution.

Thank you.

Regards,

Lalit Kumar

Cover Letter to Small Claims Complaint

25/46, Third Street
Exhibition Road,
Bangalore
06 April, 2008

Dear Sir/Madam,

Because I have had no response from you to my letters of <date> and <date>, I have had no choice but to seek relief from the court for the property damage you caused. Accordingly, I have filed a complaint with the Small Claims Court. As you will note from the complaint, this case has been scheduled for hearing on <hearing date>.

If, prior to the court's hearing date, you would like to settle this matter, I would be happy to discuss a resolution with you. If, however, I do not hear from you, or if we are unable to reach an agreeable settlement of this dispute, I am prepared to present my case to the judge.

Regards,

Lalit Kumar

Notice to Cancel Back Ordered

25/46, Third Street
Exhibition Road,
Bangalore
06 April, 2008

Dear Sir/Madam,

Please take notice that we hereby cancel our <order/contract> <order ID>, for <description of goods>, which we understand to be <back-ordered/delayed>.

Please adjust the balance in account accordingly.

Regards,

Lalit Kumar

Formal Demand Property Damage

25/46, Third Street
Exhibition Road,
Bangalore
06 April, 2008

Hello,

On 15th of March, 2008 I mailed you a letter asking that you pay the cost of repairing the damage you did to my property when you vacated this. The amount of said repairs is Rs. 5,000. The return receipt I received indicates you received my letter on 20th of March, 2005. To date, I have not had any response from you.

Please consider this letter a formal demand that you remit to me Rs. 5000 in the form of a cheque made payable to my name to pay for the repairs described above. If, for some reason, you are unable to pay this amount or if you dispute my complaint, please contact me as soon as possible so we may discuss this matter. If I do not hear from you within ten days of your receipt of this letter, I will have no choice but to seek legal recourse.

I look forward to hearing from you.

Regards,

Lalit Kumar

Initial Complaint Letter Property Damage

25/46,
Third Street,
Exhibition Road,
Bangalore
06 April, 2008

Hello,

I have obtained an estimate for the repair of damage from a reliable repair person. That estimate came to Rs. 50,000.

I would appreciate if you would please provide me Rs. 50,000 in the form of a cheque made payable to my name.

I would like to get this matter resolved as quickly as possible and appreciate your prompt attention to this request.

Regards,

Lalit Kumar

Letter Accepting Liability

25/46, Third Street
Exhibition Road,
Bangalore
06 April, 2008

Hello,

I am in receipt of your demand for payment regarding the repairs to your property. I would like to apologize for the damage caused in the incident of 25th of March, 2008 and am hereby accepting full responsibility for the necessary repairs.

Accordingly, enclosed please find my cheque made payable to your name in the amount of Rs. 10,000 to cover the cost of said repairs. If I can be of further assistance in this matter, please do not hesitate to contact me.

Regards,

Lalit Kumar

Letter Acknowledging Payment of Small Claims Judgement case Closed

25/46, Third Street
Exhibition Road,
Bangalore
06 April, 2008

Hello,

I am in receipt of your cheque in the amount of Rs. 1,00,000. <action you have taken to have the property repaired> and I consider this matter to be closed. No further legal action needs or will be taken. I appreciate your cooperation in successfully settling this dispute.

Regards,

Lalit Kumar

Letter Confirming Payment Plan

25/46, Third Street
Exhibition Road,
Bangalore
06 April, 2008

Hello,

This letter is to confirm our agreement regarding payment for the property damage you have suffered. I understand that the total cost of repairs to your property is Rs. 20,000. Pursuant to our agreement, I will pay for said repairs.

Thank you for your cooperation and assistance in getting this matter resolved. If you have any questions about this payment plan, or if the plan I have set forth does not represent your understanding of our agreement, please contact me immediately.

Regards,

Pawan Kumar

Letter Confirming Property Damage Claim

25/46, Third Street
Exhibition Road,
Bangalore
06 April, 2008

Hello,

I am in receipt of your letter dated 2nd April, 2008. Please be advised that I dispute that I am liable for the damage you allege I caused. Accordingly, I will not be paying for the repairs referenced in your letter.

If you would like to discuss this matter further, please do not hesitate to contact me.

Regards,

Pawan Kumar

Plaintiffs Requesting Payment Per Small Claims Judgement

25/46, Third Street
Exhibition Road, Bangalore
06 April, 2008

Hello,

On 27th of March, 2008 this matter was heard by Judge Mr. Sudhakar Ramamurthy in his chamber on the Small Claims Court. At that time Judge Mr. Sudhakar Ramamurthy considered our case and ruled that judgement in the amount of Rs. 50,000 be awarded to plaintiff.

Accordingly, I would appreciate if you would remit the amount of the judgement to me in the form of a cashier's cheque as soon as possible. If, after 30 days from the date of the judgement, I have not heard from you or received payment, I will seek an order from the court garnishing your wages until said judgement has been paid in full. I look forward to your prompt response.

Regards,

Lalit Kumar

Letter Enclosing Payment of Small Claims Judgement

25/46, Third Street
Exhibition Road, Bangalore
06 April, 2008

Re: Adjustment for small claims

Small Claims case No. 25478

Hello,

Please find enclosed a cheque number 5647892 made payable to your name in the amount of Rs. 20,000. This cheque represents full and final settlement of the small claims judgement entered on 30th of March, 2008. The negotiation of this instrument will terminate any further obligation on my part in this matter.

Regards,

Jagdish Chandra

■

(22)

Hotel, Airline and Travel Letters

Complaint for Lost Luggage

D-21, Street No. 3
Main Commercial Area,
Hyderabad
01 April, 2008

Dear Sir/Madam,

On a flight at 8.30 A.M. three of us were booked on flight no. AC- 456 for Hyderabad, flying out of Indira Gandhi Airport in New Delhi. Upon arrival in Hyderabad, we discovered that our luggage had been lost.

To date, we have not received any sort of compensation from Indian Airlines for the cost of our lost luggages. I would like to speak with someone as soon as possible about resolving this unpleasant situation. You may reach me at my phone number 256789.

Thank you for your attention to this matter.

Regards,

Jagdish Chandra

Complaint for Overbooked Flight

D-21, Street No. 3
Main Commercial Area, Hyderabad
01 April, 2008

Dear Sir/Madam,

<time of flight> I was booked on flight <flight number> for <destination>, flying out of

<airport name>. As it turned out, the flight was overbooked, which caused some problems that have yet to be resolved.

Please have someone from <airline name> contact me as soon as possible to resolve this matter. Thank you.

Regards,

Lalit Kumar

Complaint for Overcharged Hotel Stay

D-21, Street No. 3
Main Commercial Area,
Hyderabad
01 April, 2008

Dear Sir/Madam,

Three of us stayed at your hotel from 26th of March, 2008 to 28th of March, 2008. And while we enjoyed our stay, I realized after departing that we were overcharged for the rooms by Rs. 2000.

I believe if you check your records, you will see that we stayed for two nights in rooms that were listed at Rs. 3000. That should have brought the bill to Rs. 9000. Instead, the bill presented to us was for Rs.11,000. Please contact me as soon as possible to discuss this matter and arrange a refund or credit if necessary. Thank you for your attention to this matter.

Regards,

Lalit Kumar

Complaint of Poor Service

D-21, Street No. 3
Main Commercial Area, Hyderabad
01 April, 2008

Dear Sir/Madam,

<time of your stay>, <people who stayed at the hotel> stayed at <hotel name>. During <my/our> stay, <I/we> <was/were> very unhappy with some of the service <I/we> received.

This kind of behavior is unacceptable. Please know that <I/we> will not be staying in <hotel(s) you'll avoid> in the future. If you wish to discuss this matter with me, you may reach me at <phone number>. Thank you.

Regards,

Lalit Kumar

Complaint of Rude Flight Crew

D-21, Street No. 3
Main Commercial Area, Hyderabad
01 April, 2008

Dear Sir/Madam,

On a flight at 8.30 A.M. I was booked on flight no. AC- 456 for Hyderabad, flying out of Indira Gandhi Airport in New Delhi. I thought I should let you know that during the flight, your flight crew behaved most unprofessionally and on some occasions were downright rude.

This kind of behaviour is simply unacceptable from a professional airline. Please take steps to see that it does not happen again. If you wish to contact me about this matter, you can reach me at my phone number 2356478.

Thank you for your time.

Regards,

Pawan Kumar

Complaint of Unpleasant Room

D-21, Street No. 3
Main Commercial Area,
Hyderabad
01 April, 2008

Dear Sir/Madam,

We three people stayed at your hotel. During our stay, we found that our rooms were not comfortable at all. There were several problems regarding bed, quilt, room services etc.

I believe that due to the unsatisfactory nature of this experience, we are entitled to some sort of compensation, be it a refund or some complimentary nights at your hotel.

Please contact me as soon as possible at 2547896 about remedying this most unsatisfactory situation.

Thank you for your time and attention.

Regards,

Karma Kapoor

Complimenting Great Flight Crew

D-21, Street No. 3
Main Commercial Area,
Hyderabad
01 April, 2008

Dear Sir/Madam,

<time of flight>, <people flying> <was/were> booked on flight <flight number> for <destination>, flying out of <airport name>. I thought I should let you know that the crew on this flight was among the finest I have ever seen.

<airline name> is to be commended for employing such outstanding professionals. Rest assured you will be my airline of choice for the future. Thank you.

Regards,

Lalit Kumar

Complimenting for Good Service

D-21, Street No. 3
Main Commercial Area,
Hyderabad
01 April, 2008

Dear Sir/Madam,

<time of your stay>, <people who stayed at the hotel> stayed at <hotel name>. I just thought

I should write to let you know that <I/we> enjoyed <my/our> stay more than any time in recent memory thanks to the outstanding service we received.

Thank you for providing <me/us> with a wonderful experience. Rest assured, <I/we> will be back again.

Regards,

Lalit Kumar

Complaint to Tour Company

D-21, Street No. 3
Main Commercial Area,
Hyderabad
01 April, 2008

Dear Sir/Madam,

We took a packaged tour through your agency. We were very dissatisfied with the quality of the tour, and would like to inform you of the problems.

I feel that the tour was badly misrepresented by your agency, and I think we are entitled to some sort of compensation, such as a partial refund.

Please contact me as soon as possible to discuss how we may resolve this unpleasant situation.

Thank you for your attention to this matter.

Regards,

Lalit Kumar

Complaint to Tour Agency

D-21, Street No. 3
Main Commercial Area,
Hyderabad
01 April, 2008

Dear Sir/Madam,

<time you dealt with agency> <travelers> arranged <arrangements> through <agency name>. <I/We> <was/were> most unhappy with the results of that booking. I feel that <I/We> <was/

were> treated very poorly by <agency name>, and I think <I/We> <am/are> entitled to some sort of compensation. Please contact me as soon as possible to discuss how we may resolve this unpleasant situation.

Thank you for your attention to this matter.

Regards,

Lalit Kumar

Complaint to Travel Guidebook

D-21, Street No. 3
Main Commercial Area,
Hyderabad
01 April, 2008

Dear Sir/Madam,

I understand that it's difficult to keep your guidebooks up-to-date on every facet of every country from year to year, but the kind of glaring errors that we found on our trip to Australia are pretty hard to take.

We use travel guides frequently on our trips around the world. If you would like us to continue using yours, I would suggest you make an effort to keep the information current.

Thank you.

Regards,

Pawan Kumar

Compliment to Tour Company

D-21, Street No. 3
Main Commercial Area,
Hyderabad
01 April, 2008

Dear Sir/Madam,

<time you took tour> <travelers> took <kind of tour> through <agency name>. <I/We> <was/were> absolutely thrilled with the tour, and I thought I should write to compliment you

on your excellence. Without question, <I/We> feel that <my/our> experience on this tour was worth every penny of the money paid for it. Thank you for a wonderful time.

Regards,

Lalit Kumar

Compliment to Travel Agency

D-21, Street No. 3
Main Commercial Area,
Hyderabad
01 April, 2008

Dear Sir/Madam,

The tour you arranged for us in the shortest possible time was fantastic. We were very pleased with the work of your company, and I thought I should write to express my satisfaction.

It's a pleasure to work with a travel agency that seems so committed to meeting the needs of the customer. Thank you again, and I look forward to doing business with you in the future.

Regards,

Dhiraj Kumar

Complimenting Cabin Steward

D-21, Street No. 3
Main Commercial Area,
Hyderabad
01 April, 2008

Dear Sir/Madam,

The last tour we took on your cruise was simply amazing. On that cruise, our cabin steward named Sanjay was simply wonderful, and made us feel pampered and completely taken care of.

We thought it was completely appropriate to contact your company and let you know what an incredible job Sanjay is doing. Employees like him are a credit to your company.

Regards,

Dhiraj Kumar

Recommendation of Travel Guidebook

D-21, Street No. 3
Main Commercial Area,
Hyderabad
01 April, 2008

Dear Sir/Madam,

We recently returned from a trip to Goa, and we found something that you simply must include in the next edition of your travel guidebook. That information has been attached in a separate copy.

I hope this information will be of some use. If you would like more information on what we found, you can contact me at my phone number 254689.

Thank you for your time.

Regards,

Lalit Kumar

■

23

Real Estate Letters

Complaint About Home Inspection

C- 67/8,
Commercial Plaza,
Main Industrial Road,
Ludhiana
01 April, 2008

Dear Sir/Madam,

On 28th of February, 2008 the inspecting party came to inspect my property at D-12, Sector- 18, Ludhiana before I purchased it. At the time, I was told that the property was in good condition. In the time since that inspection and the purchase, that has not proven to be the case.

I believe that this is not the type of service a customer should expect from a professional inspection company. I would like to discuss this matter and want to take desired action. Please contact me as soon as possible to discuss this matter.

Thank you for your time.

Regards,

Gaurav Kalra

Complaint About Property Taxes

C- 67/8,
Commercial Plaza,
Main Industrial Road,
Ludhiana
01 April, 2008

Dear Sir/Madam,

A new assessment was made of my home for property taxes. When I got the results of this assessment, I was outraged, to say the least. I consider this assessment to be unfair and incorrect.

I would like to talk with the assessor or another responsible person at the assessment committee and discuss how to resolve this misunderstanding. Please call me at my phone number 256478.

Thank you for your attention to this matter.

Regards,

Lalit Kumar

Complaint of Bad Advice on Pricing Your Property

C- 67/8,
Commercial Plaza,
Main Industrial Road,
Ludhiana
01 April, 2008

Dear Sir/Madam,

When I came to you to sell my home at J block, Ludhiana, I was under the impression that you knew the pricing of comparable homes in the J block area, and that you could help me price my home to attract buyers and also get maximum value.

However, as the property has gone on the market, I have discovered that my property is terribly underpriced.

I need to meet with you immediately to discuss this problem. Please contact me at 2564789. In the meantime, I trust that you will put in the time and research necessary to price my home properly without delay.

Regards,

Lalit Kumar

Complaint About Real Estate Agent

C- 67/8,
Commercial Plaza,
Main Industrial Road,
Ludhiana
01 April, 2008

Dear Sir/Madam,

I worked with one of your agent named Mr. Sandeep Kumar for some of my property work. When I worked with this agent, I was very surprised and disappointed. I believe that this is not the type of service a customer should expect from a real estate professional. I would like to work with your company, but it will have to be with a different agent. We would appreciate hearing your thoughts on this matter.

Thank you.

Regards,

Jatin Kumar

Complaint to Builder About Problems with New House

C- 67/8,
Commercial Plaza,
Main Industrial Road, Ludhiana
01 April, 2008

Dear Sir/Madam,

I purchased a new home in your recently completed colony. At the time, the property seemed perfect, and I was thrilled to buy a new home that was, supposedly, in perfect condition.

However, since the close of the sale, many problems have arisen which should not be appearing in a brand-new home.

These sort of problems should not be occurring in a new home that was built with any standards of quality. Please contact me immediately to discuss repairs. I trust you will give this matter your full attention.

Thank you.

Regards,

Lalit Kumar

Thanks Letter to the Buyer of Your Home

C- 67/8,
Commercial Plaza,
Main Industrial Road,
Ludhiana
01 April, 2008

Dear Sir/Madam,

I just wanted to drop you a line and thank you for buying our home, and for being so wonderful to work with. Selling was not something I was looking forward to, because of all the complications and hassles that inevitably arise. But working with you made the entire experience much easier.

I wish you the best of luck in your new home, and hope that you will get as much joy from living there as I did for 5 years.

Thank you for everything.

Regards,

Pawan Kumar

Thanks Letter to the Seller of Your Home

C- 67/8,
Commercial Plaza,
Main Industrial Road,
Ludhiana
01 April, 2008

Dear Sir/Madam,

I just wanted to drop you a line and thank you for selling me your beautiful home, and for being so wonderful to work with. Buying a home was not something I was looking forward to, because of all the complications and hassles that inevitably arise. But working with you made the entire experience much easier.

I hope to get as much joy out of living in this home as you did while you were here, and we thank you for your honesty, your courtesy, and your kindness.

Best of luck in the future.

Regards,

Lalit Kumar

■

(24)

Online Service Letters

Complaint: Online Service Censors Content

12/34, Main Street
Bangalore
01 April, 2008

Dear Sir/Madam,

I became a customer of your company four years back, and have had no problems with your online service. However, I recently tried to access Web sites dealing with some of my choices and was told that the system would access those kind of sites. This seems to be censorship, plain and simple.

I am an adult, and completely capable of deciding what material I want to see and what material I wish to avoid. Since there are many software products available now which allow parents to control what areas of the Web their children can view, there seems to be no reason why your company should need to censor its service.

Please contact me and explain why you feel the need to censor what your customers may see online. I will use this information to decide whether or not I wish to remain a customer of your company.

Thank you for your time.

Regards,

Pawan Kumar

Complaint: Billing Problem

12/34, Main Street
Bangalore
01 April, 2008

Dear Sir/Madam,

I became a customer of your company for the last five years, and have had no problems with your online service. However, I recently used your online service and found a charge of Rs. 50 for using this service, which is much higher than normal.

I suspect that this bill may be in error. I have not used your service any more than in past months, and there seems to be no reason for this excessive charge. Please have someone from your Collections department contact me as soon as possible to resolve this situation.

Thank you for your time.

Regards,

Pawan Kumar

Complaint: Cancelling Online Service

12/34, Main Street
Bangalore
01 April, 2008

Dear Sir/Madam,

I became a customer of your company three years back. While I have found your service useful, I must inform you that I am cancelling my account, effective immediately.

I thank you for your services in the past. Please cancel my account immediately.

Thank you for your kind attention.

Regards,

Lalit Kumar

Complaint: Can't Dial into Online Service

12/34, Main Street
Bangalore

01 April, 2008

Dear Sir/Madam,

I became a customer of your company for the last five years, and have had no problems with your online service. However, I have recently experienced constant problems dialing into your system, problems which keep me from getting online most of the time.

Not being able to access your service is real hardship. Please contact me with any suggestions you may have about getting online more easily.

I look forward to hearing from you. Thank you for your time.

Regards,

Akash Gupta

Complaint: Can't Reach Customer Service

12/34, Main Street
Bangalore
01 April, 2008

Dear Sir/Madam,

I became a customer of <company name> <time you became a customer>, and have had no problems with your <Internet/online> service. However, I recently realized that whenever I have had problems with the service in the past, I have <never/rarely> been able to speak to a customer service or technical support person at <company name> because they are always busy.

I'm thrilled that <company name> is growing so fast, but don't you think you should be adding customer service and tech support staff to handle the additional customers? I would like to speak with someone to discuss how this problem may be handled and to find out how I can get the help I need when I need it. Please contact me at your earliest convenience.

Thank you.

Regards,

Lalit Kumar

Complaint: Online Service is too Expensive

12/34, Main Street
Bangalore

01 April, 2008

Dear Sir/Madam,

I became a customer of <company name> <time you became a customer>, and have had no problems with your <Internet/online> service. However, I have been taking a look at my bill recently, and <company name>'s service seems to be much more expensive than the competition. I would like to know why this is the case.

Most online services charge <typical fee>. My fees for using <company name>, however, have been reaching <fee you've been paying> per month, which seems excessive.

I would like some explanation of your pricing structure and why you feel you need to <online company action>. Please contact me and provide me with that information. I would like to remain a customer of <company name>, but I need information to make the proper decision.

Thank you for your time.

Regards,

Lalit Kumar

Complaint: Cut Off from Online Service

12/34, Main Street
Bangalore
01 April, 2008

Dear Sir/Madam,

I became a customer of your company five years back, and have had no problems with your online service. However, I have recently experienced constant problems being cut off suddenly in the middle of an online session. This type of constant cutoff is a major inconvenience, and I'm concerned that it might be a case of loose connection in the line. Please contact me and let me know if there is something I can do to prevent these cutoffs from happening again.

Thank you very much.

Regards,

Lalit Kumar

■

25

Miscellaneous Letters

Proposal for Industry Focus Group

25/46, Main Street
Bangalore

Dear Sir/Madam,

At ABC Company, we realize that vendor and client feedback is becoming more and more critical to doing business efficiently. After all, if we don't know what our customers want, we can't give them the products and services they need. That's why I'm writing to ask if <other company name> would be interested in helping organize a focus group for a selection of <your industry> vendors and client companies.

What I'm proposing is this: <description of focus group>. All you would need to do is contact some of your vendors and clients and find a few who are interested in having their views heard.

<work you need from the other party>.

I think such a focus group will let our vendors and clients know that ABC Company and <other company name> are committed to serving their needs, and will be a genuine avenue to greater profitability.

I will give you a call <time you will call> to talk over the matter further and see if we can get this together. Thanks for your attention.

Regards,

Lalit Kumar

Pooling Advertising Resources

25/46, Main Street
Bangalore

Dear Sir/Madam,

You know the costs of printing materials, running advertisements in the newspapers, and sending out direct mail. It's expensive. But I've got a potential solution. I have been very impressed with ABC Ltd. over the years, with your professionalism and your vision. So I would like to suggest that we make the most of our revenue and pool our advertising rupees.

By doing things like this, we could increase our bargaining power and cut better deals with local vendors and media outlets. This seems like a natural way to get more for our advertising budgets, and I can think of no other company with whom I would rather work. If you're interested in discussing the possibilities, give me a call at 589745. I look forward to speaking with you.

Regards,

Dhiraj Kumar

Proposal for Consumer Proposal Group

25/46, Main Street
Bangalore

Dear Sir/Madam,

At ABC Company, we realize that customer feedback is becoming more and more critical to doing business efficiently. After all, if we don't know what our customers want, we can't serve them, can we? That's why I'm writing to ask you if you would be interested in helping organize a focus group for some local customers.

What I'm proposing is ver simple and I can tell you this over phone. All you would need to do is make a few calls and find some interested customers.

I think such a focus group will really give both our businesses a clear idea of how to best serve our customers and become more profitable. I will give you a call to talk over the matter further and see if we can get this together. Thanks for your attention

Regards,

Lalit Kumar

Request for Event Planning Help

25/46, Main Street
Bangalore

Dear Sir/Madam,

I believe that our businesses have to stick together when it comes to promotions. That's why I'm writing for your assistance. As you may know, <company name> is putting together <event name>, to be held <event date> at <event location>. This will be an opportunity to meet many members of the community and generate a tremendous amount of positive press coverage. That's why we would like to get <other company name> on board as an organizer.

There's a lot to do, but there are also plenty of benefits from being part of <event name>, from great public relations to a lot of fun for your employees. At this point, we're looking for a company that can <describe needed work> If that sounds like something your people can handle, we'd love to have you on board. If you'd like to be part of <event name>, give me a call at <phone number> and let's work out the details. I look forward to working with you and your staff. Thanks!

Regards,

Lalit Kumar

Request for Inclusion on the Website

25/46, Main Street
Bangalore

Dear Sir/Madam,

Recently, while cruising the Web, I found the site for <other company name> at <company website URL>, and was very impressed. You have constructed a site that is <site description>. My purpose for writing this letter is simple: I would like to place a link to Abc Company's Web site on your site.

I think users who navigate through your site would be interested in finding out more about

ABC Company. Of course, we will reciprocate by placing a link to <other company name> in a prominent position on our site. I think this would prove beneficial for everyone, allowing us all to take advantage of the power of cyberspace.

Please give me a call at <phone number> or e-mail me at <e-mail address> to talk about the idea. I look forward to hearing from you.

Regards,

Sahil Seth

Follow up to Strategic Alliance Letter

25/46, Main Street

Bangalore

Dear Sir/Madam,

On 21st September, 2007, I sent you a letter proposing a strategic alliance between ABC Company and XYZ Ltd.. To date, I have not received a reply from you regarding this important matter. In case the first letter was mislaid or you've simply been too busy to respond, I thought I would contact you again.

Of course, you may simply have reservations about teaming with a company that you may have seen as a competitor. Please be assured that I and ABC Company want nothing more than for both our companies to thrive and profit. We feel that by Strategic alliance, both our companies will benefit.

I trust you can see the obvious benefits of this sort of arrangement.

Please take the time to call me at 2456789 and set up a meeting. I'll explain our ideas and show you how everyone will be thrilled with an alliance between ABC Company and <other company name>. I hope to hear from you soon.

Regards,

Lalit Kumar

Offer of Strategic Alliance

25/46, Main Street
Bangalore

Dear Sir/Madam,

It seems clear that ABC Company and XYZ Company share many of the same goals. And since two companies working together are immeasurably stronger than two companies competing, I'd like to propose a strategic alliance.

I would like to meet with you to discuss combining our efforts to for strategic alliance. I think that by working together, we could increase market share for both companies and build a very profitable long-term relationship.

If you're interested in the possibilities, please give me a call at 2346782 as soon as possible. We can arrange a time to sit down and set up what could be a very profitable, enjoyable alliance. I look forward to hearing from you.

Regards,

Lalit Kumar

Thanks Letter for Agreeing to Alliance

25/46, Main Street
Bangalore

Dear Sir/Madam,

It's a real pleasure to work with visionary, forward-thinking people! I just wanted to thank you for agreeing to bring XYZ Ltd. as part of a strategic alliance with ABC Company.

In the coming weeks, we will meet many more times to <planned actions>. I expect many more ideas to come out of these meetings, keeping us all busy for months to come.

Thanks again for taking such bold action. I'll be calling you <time you'll be calling> to set up the initial meetings and discuss some other details. I look forward to great things for <other company name> and ABC Company. Thanks again.

Regards,

Lalit Kumar

Complaint about Car Salesman

25/46, Main Street
Bangalore
01 April, 2008

Dear Sir/Madam,

On 29th of March, 2008, I came to look for a new vehicle at your showroom. I was met by a salesman named Sandeep Kumar, who, over the next half an hour gave me one of the most unpleasant sales experiences of my life.

This kind of behaviour is inexcusable, and has certainly convinced me never to shop for a car again. I thought you should know about the terrible treatment your customers are getting, so that something can be done before you lose all your business. Thank you.

Regards,

Pawan Kumar

Complimenting Auto Repair

25/46, Main Street
Bangalore
01 April, 2008

Dear Sir/Madam,

On 20th of October, 2008 I brought my car to your garage for some kind of repair work. I was helped by Ravi. I wanted to thank you and congratulate Ravi for doing a wonderful job on my car.

It's all to common to find auto repair businesses that take advantage of their customers and provide sub par service. Thank you very much for being one of the good ones. You've got a customer for life.

Regards,

Pawan Kumar

Complimenting Car Salesman

25/46, Main Street
Bangalore
01 April, 2008

Dear Sir/Madam,

<date or day of visit> <people who went shopping> came to <name> to look for a new vehicle. <I/We> <was/were> met by <salesman name>, who proceeded to take <me/us> through one of the most pleasant and informative car buying experiences I can remember.

It's all too common to run into obnoxious car salesman who only want to get your signature and their commission as fast as possible. <salesman name> proved to be a wonderful exception to that cliche, and he has ensured that <I/We> will be coming back to your dealership for years to come. Thank you very much.

Regards,

Pawan Kumar

Question about Used Car

25/46, Main Street
Bangalore
01 April, 2008

Dear Sir/Madam,

<date of purchase> I purchased your <vehicle name, year, etc.>. I have since had a few problems with the car, and I was wondering if you could give me some answers.

I know there are always risks in buying a used car. I would just like to find out what I'm dealing with and get it taken care of as soon as possible. Please give me a call at <phone number>.

Thanks for your help.

Regards,

Lalit Kumar

Acknowledge Return of Credit or Refund

25/46, Main Street
Bangalore

Dear Sir/Madam,

We are sorry that the product being returned is not what you are looking for.

I regret that we couldn't meet your needs this time but look forward to serving you in the future.

Regards,

Lalit Kumar

Acknowledging Change of Product

25/46, Main Street
Bangalore

Dear Sir/Madam,

This letter acknowledges receipt of returned merchandise. We understand that you would like to exchange it for the desired new merchandise.

If you have any questions, please call us at 254789.

Thank you for choosing ABC Company.

Regards,

Lalit Kumar

Customer Overpaid Invoice

25/46, Main Street
Bangalore

Dear Sir/Madam,

We have received your payment of Rs. 50,000 on invoice number 28572. Because <reason for overpayment> you are due a credit of Rs. 20,000.

If you have any questions, please feel free to call us at 2327852.

Regards,

Lalit Kumar

Early Payment Discount

25/46, Main Street

Bangalore

Dear Sir/Madam,

Enclosed is our invoice for <what invoice is for>. We want to remind you about our early payment discount. If we receive payment <time deadline>, we will discount the total amount due by <amount of discount>.

We hope you are able to take advantage of this discount. We look forward to serving you in the future.

Regards,

Lalit Kumar

Customer Underpaid Invoice

25/46, Main Street
Bangalore

Dear Sir/Madam,

We have received your payment of <amount> on invoice number <invoice number>. Because <reason for underpayment>, you still show a balance owed of <amount>.

If you have any questions, please feel free to call us at <phone number>. Thank you for your prompt attention to this matter.

Regards,

Lalit Kumar

Late Payment Received

25/46, Main Street
Bangalore

Dear Sir/Madam,

This is to acknowledge that we received your payment of Rs. 25,000 on invoice number 54879. Unfortunately, it was one week late. Our policy states that payment must be made within 15 days.

In a business our size we're constantly forced to monitor cash flow. In order to maintain the quality of products or services we provide, we must pay our suppliers, often before we can serve you.

In the future, we must require that you pay for all products/services in advance. We will be happy to review our position after some time.

Thank you for your understanding.

Regards,

Jagdish Kumar

Invoice Cover Letter

25/46, Main Street
Bangalore

Dear Sir/Madam,

Thank you for giving ABC Company the opportunity to serve you.

Enclosed is our invoice for the product you ordered.

Please let us know if you have any questions regarding this invoice. We look forward to serving you in the future.

Regards,

Lalit Kumar

Return Good not Returned

25/46, Main Street
Bangalore

Dear Sir/Madam,

We have received your inquiry about <description of merchandise> and find that we have no record of it. I suggest that you contact your shipper to try and trace the lost <type of merchandise>. Unfortunately, we cannot be responsible for returned merchandise that is lost in transit.

If we can be of further service, or if you get more information, please call me and I will take action from this end. I'm sorry that the <type of merchandise> did not meet your needs and that <it is/they are> now lost. We value your business and want to help any way we can.

Regards,

Lalit Kumar

Credit Approval Letter

25/46, Main Street
Bangalore

Dear Sir/Madam,

Welcome! We are pleased to inform you that your application for credit with ABC Company has been approved. We are pleased to have you as our customer.

Your credit is approved up to Rs. 1,00,000.

If you have any questions please feel free to call our credit office at 245698. We look forward to serving you in the future.

Regards,

Lalit Kumar

Credit Refusal Letter

25/46, Main Street
Bangalore

Dear Sir/Madam,

Thank you for taking the time to apply for credit with ABC Company. We welcome your business but unfortunately we are unable to extend credit to you at this time. Your credit application was denied because of some technical reasons.

When your situation changes, we would be happy to reconsider your application. In the meantime, we welcome the opportunity to do business with you on a cash basis.

Regards,

Lalit Kumar

Requesting Commercial Credit

25/46, Main Street
Bangalore

Dear Sir/Madam,

We are impressed with your products/services and would very much like to do business with you. However, before we place our initial order, we would like to inquire about your terms for granting commercial credit.

ABC Company is a big company which is a market leader in its category.

Would you please send us any information you may have, as well as the necessary forms or credit applications? Thank you. We look forward to doing business with you.

Regards,

Dhiraj Kumar

Ask Customer to Complete Credit Application

25/46, Main Street
Bangalore

Dear Sir/Madam,

We are very pleased that you have decided to do business with ABC Company and look forward to serving you in the future. Before we can establish a credit account, we require all new customers to complete the enclosed credit application. Once we receive the completed form, we can set up your credit account.

You should hear about your credit approval with in 2 weeks. If you have any questions about the application or our approval process, please call me at 5689255. Thank you for deciding to do business with ABC Company.

Regards,

Lalit Kumar

Cancel Stop Payment

25/46, Main Street
Bangalore
05 April, 2008

Dear Sir/Madam,

You are hereby requested to cancel the previous stop-payment request on the cheque referenced below and to honor and pay it from our account number 214578 when it is next presented.

Cheque Number: 5478965 Cheque Date: 12th of March, 2008

Amount: Rs. 55,000 Payee: Mr. Sidharth

Thank you for your assistance in this matter.

Regards,

Lalit Kumar

Demand for Payment of Promissory Note

25/46, Main Street
Bangalore
05 April, 2008

Dear Sir/Madam,

As the holder of your promissory note dated 20th of March, 2008, we hereby demand payment of the unpaid balance of principal and accrued interest in the amount of Rs. 65,000. We expect to receive full payment by 30th of April, 2008. If you anticipate any trouble making this payment, please contact us immediately.

Thank you for your prompt attention to this request.

Regards,

Pawan Kumar

Notice of Default on Promissory Note

25/46, Main Street
Bangalore
05 April, 2008

Dear Sir/Madam,

We hold your promissory note dated <date of note> in the amount of <original amount>. We hereby give you notice that you are in default on said note for failure to pay the following <amounts/installments>:

- <list of overdue payments>

Accordingly, we hereby demand payment of <total amount of demand>.

If we have not received payment as specified above <payment address> by <payment deadline>, we shall turn this matter over to collection at your expense, as provided for in said note.

Regards,

Lalit Kumar

Landlord Letter of Complaint Received

25/46, Main Street
Bangalore
05 April, 2008

Hello,

Please be advised that on 20th of March, 2008, I received a complaint about your behaviour in the society. This letter is to place you on notice that this is a serious problem which needs to be addressed. Please immediately desist from doing this things in your neighbourhood.

If, perhaps there has been some misunderstanding, I would appreciate you notifying me at once. Otherwise, I trust that I will receive no additional complaints in this regard in the future.

Regards,

Dhiraj Kumar

Notice of Late Rent

25/46, Main Street
Bangalore
05 April, 2008

Hello,

Please be advised that your rent payments for the last two months have fallen in arrears. As of the date of this notice, the following payments are now past due:

Rents for the months of February and March, 2008. Pursuant to our Rental Agreement, unless you cure this default on your payments, I will be forced to ask you to immediately vacate the property you are living in. Please contact me as soon as possible to discuss payment options and to avoid potential legal problems.

Thank you.

Regards,

Lalit Kumar

Notice of Termination of Lease

25/46, Main Street
Bangalore
05 April, 2008

Hello,

Pursuant to the provisions of our Lease agreement dated <lease date>, I have elected to terminate said lease as of <date of termination>. This termination <reason(s) for termination>, and you are hereby required to quit and deliver up possession of the <item> on or before <date of termination>.

Regards,

Lalit Kumar

Notice to Pay Rent or Vacate

25/46, Main Street
Bangalore
05 April, 2008

Hello,

You are hereby given notice that under the term of that lease dated <date> between <landlord> as Lessor, and yourself as Lessee, for the premises known as <Full address of leased property>, you are in default of said Lease for certain reasons.

In the event of your failure to either cure said defaults or vacate the premises covered under said Lease within grace period from and after your receipt of this Notice, you shall be in unlawful detainer of said premises.

In the event of your failure to either cure said defaults or vacate the premises by said date, you shall be subject to Lessor's rights to commence an action for unlawful detainer as provided by applicable law. In any such action, Lessor shall seek both possession of the premises and monetary damages, including prejudgement interest on each of the amounts set forth above, double the amount of rent past due, attorneys fees and costs.

Should it be necessary to evict you and your property remains on the premises, please be advised that the law allows that Lessor shall be entitled to reasonable storage costs of your property until such property may be removed.

In order to cure these defaults you must, within the time set forth in this Notice, pay all sums set forth above to Lessor by tender to Lessor at <full address of lessor>.

Regards,

Lalit Kumar

Notice to Vacate

25/46, Main Street
Bangalore
05 April, 2008

Hello,

Take notice that our lease agreement is terminated and that your tenancy of the premises described therein is hereby terminated at the expiration of time period after receipt of this notice. You are hereby required to vacate the premises and deliver possession of the premises now held and occupied by you under such tenancy.

This is intended as a time period notice to quit, for the purpose of terminating your tenancy aforesaid.

Regards,

Lalit Kumar

Change of Address Awaiting Refund

Dear Satish,

Your correspondence, dated April 15, 2007 indicated that I would be receiving a refund for the unused portion of prorated insurance coverage provided under the above referenced policy.

As of this date, I have not yet received this cheque. Since I have moved, I am naturally concerned that the cheque may have been sent to the wrong address.

Would you please let me know if a cheque has been mailed.

Thank you for your attention to this matter. My new address is attached with this letter once again for your convenience.

Yours,

Kunal Dasgupta

Collateral Decision, Request for Preparation of Loan Documents

Dear Lalit,

It was a pleasure having the opportunity to meet with you yesterday to discuss the proposed loan.

I am instructing my secretary to prepare a package consisting of all necessary documents and to mail them to your attention today. I would be most appreciative if you would arrange to have the loan documents drawn as soon as possible.

I wish to thank you for your cooperation in this matter and am looking forward to the continuance of a long and mutually beneficial relationship between us.

Yours,

Siddharth Singh

Commendation and Refusal of Request for Raise

Dear Deepak,

This is to acknowledge your letter of 6th August. You are definitely to be commended for your progress during the past two months.

I do believe, however, that your recent request for a raise is premature. I would suggest that it would be more appropriate to discuss a salary increase after you have worked here for six months. If you continue on the same path, I am certain that your timely request will be given careful consideration.

You are doing a fine job, keep up the good work!

Yours,

Anurag Basu

Company Bonus Letter

Dear Hem,

The presentation you prepared for the current project was truly outstanding. There is no doubt that we were awarded this project due to your fine work.

Please accept the enclosed cheque as our way of saying thank you for a job well done.

Yours,

Abhishek Kumar

Agreement to Extend Debt Payment

For value received, the undersigned, and Company, hereby acknowledge and agree that:

1. The Company presently owes the Creditor the sum of Rs. 50 Lakh, said sum being presently due and payable.
2. In further consideration of the Creditor's forbearance, the Company agrees to pay said debt on extended terms.
3. In the event the Company fails to make any payments punctually on the agreed extended terms, the Creditor shall have full rights to proceed for the collection of the entire balance then remaining.
4. This agreement shall be binding upon and inure to the benefit of the parties, their successors, assigns and personal representatives.

Signed under seal

Monday, 21st March, 2008

Aakash Srivastava

(Creditor)

Recommendation Regarding Repaired Product

Dear John,

The repairs to your product have been completed and you should be receiving your product within the next few days.

We would like to recommend you some suggestions to ensure the long life of this product. By following this simple procedure, you will eliminate the chance of this problem happening again. We would like to take this opportunity to thank you for choosing our product. We will look forward to being able to be of service to you in the future and hope that you will keep our company in mind when you are selecting a new product.

Thank you again for your patronage.

Yours,

Satish Kumar

Assignment of Contract

For value received, the undersigned Assignor hereby assigns, transfers and sets over to Mr. K. Kashyap (Assignee) all right, title and interest.

The Assignor warrants and represents that said contract is in full force and effect and is fully assignable. The Assignee hereby assumes and agrees to perform all obligation of the Assignor under the contract and guarantees to hold the Assignor harmless from any claim or demand made there under.

Signed under seal this Monday, 23rd of September, 2008.

K. Kumar
(Assignor)
Mr. K. Kashyap
(Assignee)

Confirmation of Extension of Payment Date

Dear Lalit,

This will acknowledge our telephone conversation on 2nd March. As was stated in our letter dated 25th February, we should be receiving our financing by 14th March, 2008.

In view of the above, we would appreciate your extending the date for our payment of the account until 21st March. This will enable us to make sure that all of the appropriate documents have been prepared.

We appreciate your courtesies, past and present. It has been a pleasure doing business with your company and we look forward to years of pleasant associations.

Yours Truly,

Manoj Kumar

Cover Letter in Response to Catalogue Request

Dear Aditya,

Thank you for your inquiry about our equipment. I am enclosing our catalogue for your review.

We developed this equipment to provide educators with a comprehensive and effective means of transmitting information and to help modernize educational methods. That children are highly receptive and stimulated to learn through the usage of audio-visual material, is widely accepted by educators throughout the field. After you have reviewed our material, we would appreciate hearing your comments, and we will look forward to answering any questions you have about our product.

Once again, thank you for your interest in the product.

Yours Truly,

Subhas Kumar

Credit Extension to Past Due Preferred Customer

Dear Karan,

Our credit department has notified me that your account is past due. You are one of our preferred customers and therefore we want to offer any assistance we can. We know that most overdue balances result from clerical errors. However, should you require additional time to settle your balance, please feel free to give us a call. I will see to it that you are granted an additional (10) days in which to pay your account balance.

We value your business, and sincerely hope that this gesture will be of some help. Thank you for your kind consideration, and we look forward to seeing you soon.

Yours,

S. K. Singh

Customer Incentive Programme Announcement

Dear Customer,

As a valued customer of our company, we couldn't wait to bring you the good news. This letter is to announce the incorporation of our new customer incentive programme. Well, maybe we haven't thought of a great logo for it yet, but if you read on I think you'll agree that no matter what we call it, it's super!

Starting on June 1st, a record of your account with our store will be maintained on a cumulative basis for a period of one year. Once your purchases have reached Rs. 5000, you will be automatically entitled to a 5% discount on any order placed, including orders for sale items. When your orders have reached the Rs.10,000 mark, your discount will increase to 10%. A Rs. 15,000 accumulation of orders will entitle you to a 15% discount and once you have reached Rs. 20,000 you will receive 20% off all merchandise orders. We think it's a great idea and hope that you agree.

Won't you send us a purchase order today to get you started on your way? If you think of a good name for us to tag onto this new discount programme, please let us know!

Yours Truly,

Sudhanshu Shekhar

Deliveries Held Until Past Due Balance Paid

Dear John,

Due to the problems we have been experiencing of late in obtaining your payment for the goods we have delivered in accordance with the provisions of our contract, we must inform you that we will not be able to deliver any more goods to you unless you provide us with adequate assurance for payment on said goods. We regret having to withhold further deliveries, but, at this point in time, we have no other viable alternative. Please let us know promptly what your decision is in regard to your willingness to provide us with the adequate assurance we are requesting.

Yours,

Ajay Kumar

Follow-Up on Release of Pending Order

Dear Laxman,

As we discussed in our recent telephone conversation, I have released your "pending" order on our terms of net 30 days, with payment expected on or before 30 days from the date of the invoice.

I appreciate your candor and am looking forward to getting your account back on sure footing in the not too distant future.

Yours,

Manoj Gaur

Good Faith Partial Payment to Creditor

Dear Subhas,

This is to inform you that I am in receipt of your letter of 2nd December, 2008 and I acknowledge that my account is in the arrears in the amount of Rs. 100,000.

We have been experiencing some difficulties lately in collecting our accounts receivable and unfortunately the domino theory has become a reality.

In fairness to all of our creditors, I would like to suggest that I send you Rs. 10,000 per month for a period of 7 months in order to satisfy this obligation. I am enclosing the first cheque for Rs. 10,000 as a sign of good faith and am hoping that this proposal will be acceptable to you. It is understood that should we be successful in our attempts to collect some of our larger receivables during the next months, I will be most happy to remit the entire balance owing on this account.

Please let me hear from you regarding the proposal I have outlined. Thank you for your patience and understanding in this regrettable situation.

Yours,

Lalit Singh

Grant of Request for Extension of Time

Dear Hem,

Thank you for your letter in which you explained the circumstances behind your request for an extension of time to remit your payment on invoice no. 2564.

We do appreciate your straightforwardness and have noted on your account that your payment will be made on 5th of August, 2008. You have been a loyal customer of ours for quite some time and if this gesture on our part helps to ease your current situation, we are pleased to be of assistance.

Yours Truly,

Pawan Kandpal

Holiday Letter to Stockholders

To our Shareholders:

We want to extend to each and everyone of you our warmest wishes for the coming holiday season.

We are enclosing the financial results for the second quarter and year to date period ending 30th of September, 2006. and hope that this "good news" will add to your holiday spirits.

May your Christmas season be filled with happiness and joy, followed by a most wonderful New Year.

Harish Sah

ABC Corporations

Initial Notice of Balance Discrepancy

Dear Bhaskar,

In your letter dated 4th of March, 2007, you have indicated that my current balance in the account is Rs. 55,000. Since this amount does not agree with my records, I am preparing an accounting to find the discrepancy.

Unfortunately, my accountant still has all of my 2007 cancelled cheques which were delivered to him for the preparation of my 2007 tax return. I have made arrangements for these cheques to be returned to me and should have a reconciliation ready for your review within the next ten days.

Once I am satisfied with the accuracy of the accounting, I will forward a letter, with any required documentation, to your attention.

Thank you for your patience and cooperation in this matter.

Yours,

Subrato Sahay

Late Payment Cover Letter

Dear Pratik,

Enclosed is our payment in the amount of Rs. 60,000 which should clear up any balance in our account with you.

We are very sorry that it has taken such a long time to remit our payment to you and we hope that you will understand that we have been experiencing some extremely difficult cash flow problems. We are happy to inform you, however, that we are now on the road to recovery and anticipate a good year.

Thank you for your understanding and the courteousness you have shown our company during this rough period.

Yours Truly,

Deepak Gera

Letter of Encouragement to Sales Staff

To: Sales Department

Dear Family Member of this company,

There are two sides to the story, two sides of a coin, and two ways to face the day.

There are always the prophets of doom and the cynics who will be happy to lead their followers through long periods of drought and famine.

When an unfortunate individual starts blaming his own failures on others, and on conditions over which he has no control, he can usually forget about achieving his goals.

There are good times and bad times, but at all times there are sales that are made and sales that are lost.

You have all proven that you are not only capable, but excel as salesmen. I am proud of the accomplishments of our sales force and know that nothing can hold back the motivated individual who has an excellent product to sell.

In the months to come, I feel confident that you will persevere in a manner that will result in an increase in sales and commissions to each and every one of you that will far exceed our projections.

The outlook for the coming year is brighter than it has been for some time. With a positive, assertive attitude, nothing can stop us!

Yours,
Jatin Prasad

Head, Sales and Marketing

Letter of Follow Up or Duplicate Order

Dear Somesh,

On May 1st of May, 2008 we ordered 100 copies of your book, "How to Write Business Letters", but we have not yet received an acknowledgment of that order.

As our first order may have gone astray, please consider this a duplicate.

Yours,

Ashutosh Sah

Letter of Understanding Regarding Terms of Proposed Contract

Dear Karan,

This will confirm that which we discussed during our telephone conversation earlier today.

It is agreed that your firm will provide the technical support for the projectwhile we will provide the technical equipment, to your specifications, and all funds necessary.

If this meets with your understanding of our conversation, please sign a copy of this letter and return it to my office. Upon our receipt of this verified letter, we will forward same to our attorneys for final contract drafting and revisions.

It was a pleasure speaking with you, and I hope to join you soon for a toast to our mutual success in the project.

Yours,

Rajnish Jha

Letter to Small Businessman in Advance of Collections

Dear Somesh,

As a good businessman, you are aware of the manner in which accounts that have become seriously past due must be handled. I am not going to attempt to think of some clever phrase or witty jingle to get your attention. Neither do I wish to embarrass, intimidate or do any of the nasty things that are often done to encourage payment.

I am merely informing you that the account has reached a point where we must decide within a few days whether to turn it over for collection or just hand it to our attorneys, neither of which is our preference.

We know that you understand our predicament and are probably experiencing a similar situation with some of your aging accounts. We would like to hear from you and learn what your intentions are in regard to this account.

Yours,

Harish Chaturvedi

Monthly Partial Payment to Creditor

Dear Jagdish,

In accordance with our agreement, I am enclosing our cheque in the amount of Rs. 20,000, which represents a minimum payment that you can expect each month from our firm. As you will note, this amount will decrease the balance owing to zero in twelve payments.

Naturally, if we can generate a cheque, either more frequently or in larger amounts, please be assured that we will. Furthermore, we are hopeful that we will be successful in collecting some of our very large receivables, which would enable us to pay the entire amount due.

Thank you for your courtesy and cooperation.

Yours,

Lalit Jain

Negative Response to Job Application

Dear Som,

Thank you for your recent application to join our company as a marketing executive.

While we do not have an opening in your area at this time, we will certainly keep your application on file. Should a position become available in the future, we shall inform you and arrange a convenient time for testing.

With good wishes

Deepak Kohli

Welcome to New Customer

Dear Gaurav,

Our firm would like to welcome you as a new customer to our firm. We know that you will be extremely satisfied with our line of products and the service we provide to our customers. You are invited to purchase our merchandise on our regular open account terms. Our credit manager will be happy to discuss any aspect of our credit policy with you at your convenience.

I am enclosing our catalogue and price list for your review. I believe that you will find our prices competitive and in keeping with industry trends. Throughout the year we offer our valued customers frequent discounts as an incentive and as a showing of our appreciation.

I do hope you will afford us the opportunity to serve you in the near future.

Yours Truly,

Rakshit Pandey

New Salesman Follow-Up Letter after First Meeting

Dear Pawan,

Thank you for affording me the opportunity to meet with you and members of your staff.

I know that Mr. Deepak Singh serviced your account for many years and made many friends at your firm. While his presence will be missed, I can promise that you will continue to receive the fine service that has always been afforded by the firm.

The hospitality you showed me yesterday explains why ex-salesman, Mr. Deepak Singh held your organisation is such high regard.

Thank you once again.

Yours,

Snehil Tripathi

Offer to Special Order Merchandise Not in Stock

Dear Lalit,

After checking with all of our other stores in the area, I regret to inform you that I have been unable to locate another item requested for you.

If you would like me to place a special order, I would be most happy to do so. Normally, it takes between four to six weeks to receive merchandise ordered in this manner. If this is your desire, please call me at your convenience at my telephone no. (011) 24578956.

On behalf of the firm I would like to thank you for shopping at our store and if there is any way that we can be of further assistance to you, please let us know.

Yours,

Manoj Karnataka

Offer of 2% Discount for Speedy Payments

Dear Akshay,

In the past twelve months you have purchased a considerable amount of merchandise from us, which pleases us greatly.

Since you have never taken advantage of the 2% discount we offer for early payment, we thought that you might be unaware of just how substantial your savings could be. The savings on last year's purchases alone would have amounted to Rs. 120,000. By paying us within 10 days of delivery, you can actually save 24% of the face amount of your average monthly bill over the period of a year.

There are, in fact, firms who prefer to borrow funds to take advantage of this discount. Of course, you know what is best for your own business, but we want to be sure that you are aware of this savings factor.

We would like to take this opportunity to thank you for the orders you have given to us over this past year and the promptness with which you have always paid. It is a pleasure doing business with your firm.

Yours Truly,

Shailendra Kumar

Overdue Payment Reminder Letter

Dear Neeraj,

Our records indicate that payment on your account is overdue in the amount of Rs. 50,000. If the amount has already been paid, please disregard this notice. If you have not yet mailed your payment, why not make out your cheque and place it in the enclosed envelope while this reminder is has your full attention.

Thank you in advance for your anticipated cooperation in this matter.

Yours,

Adesh Kumar

Party Announcement for New Product Line

Come celebrate with us!

We are previewing our new product line on Thursday, September 17, 2008. We will be waiting for you at the company's hall.

The party starts at 10:00 a. m. and continues until 10:00 p.m.

We are looking forward to seeing you there.

Personal Financial Statement

The undersigned for the purpose of procuring and establishing credit from time to time with you and further, to induce you to permit the undersigned to become indebted to you on notes, endorsements, guarantees, overdrafts or otherwise, furnishes the following (or in lieu thereof the attached).

Which is the most recent statement prepared by or for the undersigned as being a full, true and correct statement of the financial condition of the undersigned on the date indicated, and agrees to notify you immediately of the extent and character of any material change in said financial condition, and also agrees that if the undersigned, or any endorser or guarantor of any of the obligations of the undersigned, at any time fails in business or becomes insolvent, or commits an act of bankruptcy, or dies, or if a writ of attachment, garnishment, execution or other legal process be issued against property of the undersigned or if any assessment for taxes against the undersigned, other than taxes on real property, is made by the federal or state government or any department thereof, or if any of the representations made below prove to be untrue, or if the undersigned fails to notify you of any material change as above agreed, or if such change occurs, or if the business, or any interest therein, of the undersigned is sold, then and in such case, all of the obligations of the undersigned to you or held by you shall immediately be due and payable, without demand or notice.

This statement shall be construed by you to be a continuing statement of the condition of the undersigned, and a new and original statement of all assets and liabilities upon each and every transaction and by which the undersigned hereinafter becomes indebted to you, until the undersigned advises in writing to the contrary.

Date: 15th of January, 2008

Balram Kumar

(Signature)

Photo and Recording Release

For good and valuable consideration, the receipt of which is hereby acknowledged, I hereby consent to the photographing of myself and the recording of my voice and the use of these photographs and/or recordings singularly or in conjunction with other photographs and/or recordings for advertising, publicity, commercial or other business purposes. I understand that the term "photograph" as used herein encompasses both still photographs and motion picture footage.

Kunal Kapoor

(Signature)

Pledge of Personal Property as Collateral Security

For value received, the undersigned hereby deposits and pledges as collateral security to secure the payment of debt. It is understood and agreed that:

1. Pledgee may assign or transfer said debt and the pledged collateral hereunder.
2. Pledgee shall have no liability for loss, destruction or casualty to the collateral unless caused by his own negligence.

3. The undersigned shall pay any and all insurance it elects to maintain on the pledged collateral and any personal property, excise or other tax or levy.
4. The undersigned warrants that it has good title to the pledged collateral, authority to pledge same and that it is free of any adverse lien, encumbrance or claim.
5. In the event of default of payment of the debt or breach of this pledge agreement, the Pledgee or holder shall have full rights to foreclose on the pledged collateral and exercise its rights as a secured party pursuant to Articles of the constitution; said rights being cumulative with any other rights the Pledgee may have against the undersigned.

Signed under seal this Monday, 21st of November, 2008.

Ashish Kumar

(Signature)

Preferred Customer Sale Announcement

Dear Kailash,

The best time to take advantage of our low prices is now!

We have every reason to believe that at the June wholesale exhibition, the overall theme will be higher prices. With inflation talk creeping back into the news, this show provides the companies the chance to show their new merchandise—and raise prices.

Why not beat inflation and drop by soon. We are having a special Preferred Customer Sale. You will be pleased with the products; you will be amazed by some of the prices. In any event, drop by and say "hello".

Yours Truly,

Manohar Kumar

Refund for Carefully-Packaged Returned Merchandise

Dear Rajesh,

Having received the merchandise you returned to us, we are enclosing our cheque to you in the amount of Rs. 45,000. Thank you for taking such care in the packing of the returned merchandise.

We are sorry that circumstances prompted the return of this merchandise, but hope that you will continue to allow us to serve you in the future.

Yours Truly,

Manohar Singhal

Refund of Duplicate Payment

Dear Sumit,

Enclosed is our cheque in the amount of Rs. 50,000 which represents a refund for your inadvertant duplicate remittance for payment.

We are pleased that our bookkeeping department discovered this overpayment so quickly.

Thank you.
Yours Truly,

Kamal Tiwari

Refusal to Accept Late Return of Merchandise

Dear Rajesh,

Over the years we have had to formulate various company policies. These policies have never been arbitrarily adopted, but rather chosen in order to be able to accommodate our customers by providing our product at the lowest conceivable price while remaining in business.

One of these policies is that our customers have (10) days in which to return any merchandise for a full refund. We feel this allows sufficient time to inspect our product and be assured of its quality.

I am grateful for the business you have seen fit to give our firm and am proud to have you as one of our customers.

I cannot, however, authorize the return of our merchandise as you have requested.

I am sorry that I cannot accommodate you in this matter and I hope you will understand why we must take this position.

Yours,

Kaushal Singh

Second Overdue Payment Reminder

Dear Jacob,

Perhaps you have overlooked the fact, but your account with us is currently overdue. I have enclosed a statement of your account, which shows a balance due of Rs. 45,000. If there is some reason why you have failed to remit your payment, please call us, and let's discuss the problem.

If it would be more convenient, please feel free to write a note at the bottom of this letter and send it to my office in the enclosed envelope.

Thank you for your prompt attention to this matter.

Yours Truly,

Lalit Singhal

Second Request for Correction of Billing Error

Dear Sonu,

I received your letter, of 21st of February, 2008 in which you state that your records indicate my present balance owing is Rs. 25,000 which is not correct according to my record. I cancelled some of my cheques and may be this is the fact why this mistake happened.

I am enclosing a xerox copy of my cancelled cheques. I shall appreciate your prompt efforts in correcting this error in my account as soon as possible. Thank you for your early attention to this matter.

Yours Truly,

Aditya sharma

Second Request for Renewal of Service Agreement

Dear Parmod,

Your Service Agreement has expired for the equipment that we installed on your premises. We have not received a remittance or a reply to our previous request for payment. Perhaps this was an oversight on your part, or perhaps your payment is in the mail.

If you have not sent us your payment, please forward your remittance within ten days, or we will assume you do not wish to continue your Service Agreement.

Should you decide to terminate your Service Agreement, we will look forward to furnishing the same high quality service on your equipment at our currently hourly rate of Rs. 120 per hour, plus parts and travel expense.

Yours Truly,

Brajesh Sharma

Shipments Held Until Past Due Balance Paid

Dear Sanjay,

This is to confirm our recent telephone conversation regarding the past due balance of your account.

As I mentioned in our conversation, the current balance on the account is Rs. 45,000, of which Rs. 40,000 is now past due for payment. We will look forward to receiving your cheque within the next week to clear the past due charges on your account.

Once these charges have been cleared, we will be in a position to review the current credit arrangements for your account. Presently, however, all orders are currently being referred to us and your cheques to clear the past due balance must be received before future shipments on credit can be made.

Your cooperation and prompt attention to this matter will be greatly appreciated. If you have any questions regarding your account, please do not hesitate to contact me.

Yours Truly,

Sudhir Joshi

Spontaneous Good Customer Relations Letter

Dear Virender,

Call it nostalgia, if you wish, but as I was glancing over some of the accounts we have had for several years, I stopped when I arrived at the name of your firm.

It has been a long time since our very first transaction was initiated and it is with a great sense of pride that I realize how far both of our firms have come since that day so many years ago. The fact that our relationship has not only lasted, but has flourished over this period of time, is most rewarding.

Thank you for the past, for the present, and may the future be a continuance of that which was established long ago.

Yours Truly,

Ramdeen Sharma

Standard Cover Letter in Response to Inquiry

Dear Naveen,

Thank you for your recent inquiry about prices of some of our prominent products.

We are enclosing our catalogue and price list for your review and are confident that this literature will provide many of the answers you have requested.

If there is additional information you would like to have regarding our products, please do not hesitate to contact us. We will be most happy to be of assistance.

Thank you for the very kind words you used to describe our line of products.

Your faithfully

Gopal Kalra

■